The rise of
ADOLF HITLER
FROM DEMOCRACY TO DICTATOSHIP

SUSHMITA DUTTA

TRUE SIGN
PUBLISHING HOUSE

Published by True Sign Publishing House
Address: SY. No. 21/2 & 21/3, Sonnenahalli,
Krishnarajapura, Bengaluru,
Karnataka - 560049 India
E-mail: truesignbooks@gmail.com
Website: www.truesign.in

**The Rise Of Adolf Hitler
From Democracy To Dictatorship**

Author: Sushmita Dutta

ISBN: 978-93-5805-939-7

First Edition: 2023

CONTENTS

Introduction

Adolf Hitler was one of the most powerful and undisputed leaders of the 20th century. He rose to power as the leader of Germany's Nazi Party, becoming the **Chancellor** in 1933 and then taking the title of **Führer und Reichskanzler** in 1934.

In 1923, Adolf Hitler and the Nazi Party led a coalition group in an attempt to overthrow the German government. This attempted coup d'état came to be known as the **Beer Hall Putsch**. His trial brought him fame and followers. He used his jail time to dictate his political ideas in a book, **'Mein Kampf'—'My Struggle.'** Hitler's ideological goals included territorial expansion, consolidation of a racially pure state, and elimination of the European Jews and other perceived enemies of Germany.

Hitler capitalized on economic woes, popular discontent and political infighting to take absolute power in Germany beginning in 1933. During his dictatorship, he initiated World War II in Europe by invading Poland in September 1939.

As the leader of Germany's **Third Reich** in the 1930s and 1940s, Adolf Hitler developed a totalitarian fascist state dedicated to imperialist expansion of a pure German race. Hitler's virulent anti-Semitism and obsessive pursuit of Aryan supremacy fueled the genocide of some 6 million Jews, along with millions of other victims of the Holocaust.

The greatest enemy of Nazism was not, in Hitler's view, liberal democracy in Germany, which was already on the verge of collapse. It was the rival **Weltanschauung**, Marxism (which for him embraced social democracy as well as communism), with its insistence on internationalism and economic conflict. Beyond Marxism he believed the greatest enemy of all to be the Jews, who was for Hitler the incarnation of evil. In '**Mein Kampf**' he described the Jews as the "destroyer of culture," "a parasite within the nation," and "a menace."

His most amazing achievement was uniting the great mass of the German (and Austrian) people behind him. Throughout his career his popularity was larger and deeper than the popularity of the National Socialist Party. A great majority of Germans believed in him until the very end. In this respect he stands out among all the dictators of the 19th and 20th centuries.

Recognizing Germany's imminent defeat, Hitler committed suicide in Berlin on April 30th 1945. In his final will and testament, written just before his suicide in April 1945, he charged the Germans to continue the struggle against the Jews: "Above all, I enjoin the government and the people to uphold the race laws to the limit and to resist mercilessly the poisoner of all nations, international Jewry."

Chapter – 1

Early Years of Adolf Hitler

Childhood and Education

Adolf Hitler was born on April 20th 1889 in Braunau am Inn, a town in Austria-Hungary (in present-day Austria. He was the fourth of six children born to Alois Hitler and his third wife, Klara Pölzl. Three of Hitler's siblings—Gustav, Ida, and Otto—died in infancy. When Hitler was three-years-old, the family moved to Passau, Germany. There he acquired the distinctive lower Bavarian dialect, rather than Austrian-German, which marked his speech throughout his life. The family returned to Austria and settled in Leonding in 1894, and in June 1895 Alois retired to Hafeld, near Lambach, where he farmed and kept bees. Hitler attended Volksschule (a state-funded primary school) in nearby Fischlham.

The move to Hafeld coincided with the onset of intense father-son conflicts caused by Hitler's refusal to conform to the strict discipline of his school. His father beat him, although his mother tried to protect him. Alois Hitler's farming efforts at Hafeld ended in failure, and in 1897 the family moved to Lambach. The eight-year-old Hitler took singing lessons, sang in the church choir, and even considered becoming a priest.

Linz

In 1898, the family moved to Linz, the capital of Upper Austria. Hitler wanted a career in the visual arts. He fought bitterly with his father, who wanted him to enter the Habsburg civil service. After his father's death, Hitler eventually persuaded his mother, Klara Pölzl, to permit him to pursue his dream of becoming an artist. As Klara was dying of breast cancer in the autumn of 1907, Hitler took the entrance exam to the Vienna Academy of the Arts. He failed to gain acceptance. In early 1908, some weeks after Klara's death in December 1907, Hitler moved to Vienna, ostensibly in the hope of renewing efforts to enter the Academy of Arts.

Alois had made a successful career as a state customs official and wanted his son to follow in his footsteps. Hitler later dramatised an episode from this period when his father took him to visit a customs office, depicting it as an event that gave rise to an unforgiving antagonism between father and son, who were both strong-willed. Ignoring his son's desire to attend a classical high school and become an artist, Alois sent Hitler to the **Realschule** in Linz in September 1900. Hitler rebelled against this decision, and in **'Mein Kampf'** states that he intentionally did poorly in school, hoping that once his father saw "what little progress I was making at the technical school he would let me devote myself to my dream."

Like many Austrian-Germans, Hitler began to develop German nationalist ideas from a young age. He expressed loyalty only to Germany, despising the declining Habsburg monarchy and its rule over an ethnically variegated empire. Hitler and his friends used the greeting **"Heil"**, and sang the **"Deutschlandlied"** instead of the Austrian Imperial anthem.

After Alois's sudden death on 3rd January 1903, Hitler's performance at school deteriorated and his mother allowed him to leave. He enrolled at the Realschule in Steyr in September 1904, where his behaviour and performance improved. In 1905, after passing a repeat of the final exam, Hitler left the school without any ambitions for further education or clear plans for a career.

Early Adulthood in Vienna and Munich

In 1907, Hitler left Linz to live and study fine art in Vienna, financed by orphan's benefits and support from his mother. He applied for admission to the **Vienna's Academy of Fine Arts** but was rejected twice. The director suggested Hitler should apply to the School of Architecture, but he lacked the necessary academic credentials because he had not finished secondary school.

On 21st December 1907, his mother died of breast cancer at the age of 47, when he himself was 18. The young Hitler was a resentful, discontented child. Moody, lazy, of unstable temperament, he was deeply hostile towards his strict, authoritarian father and strongly attached to his indulgent, hard-working mother, whose death from cancer in December 1908 was a shattering blow to the adolescent Hitler.

After his mother, Klara, died in 1908, Hitler moved to Vienna, where he pieced together a living painting scenery and monuments and selling the images. Lonely, isolated and a voracious reader, Hitler became interested in politics during his years in Vienna, and developed many of the ideas that would shape Nazi ideology.

In 1909, Hitler ran out of money and was forced to live a bohemian life in homeless shelters and a men's dormitory. He earned money as a casual labourer and by painting and selling water colours of Vienna's sights. During his time in Vienna, he pursued a growing passion for architecture and music, attending ten performances of **Lohengrin**, his favourite Wagner opera.

Vienna

Hitler lived in Vienna between February 1908 and May 1913. He had grown up in a middle-class family, with relatively few contacts with Jewish people, in a region of the Habsburg state in which many German nationalists had been disappointed that the German Empire founded in 1871 had not included the German-speaking regions of the Habsburg monarchy. Yet, the legacy of the Vienna years is not as clear as Hitler depicted it in his political autobiography. His impoverishment and residence in homeless shelters began only a year after his arrival and after he had frittered away a generous inheritance left by his parents and rejected all arguments of surviving relatives and family friends that he embark upon a career in the civil service.

By the end of 1909, Hitler knew real poverty as his sources of income dried up. That winter, however, helped briefly by a last gift from his aunt, he began to paint watercolor scenes of Vienna for a business partner. He made enough to live on until he left for Munich in 1913.

It is likely that Hitler experienced, and possibly also shared, the general anti-semitism common among middle-class German nationalists. Nevertheless, he had personal and business relationships with Jews in Vienna. He was also, at times, dependent in part on Jews for his living. While this may have been a cause for discretion about his actual feelings about Jews, it was not until after World War I that Hitler can be demonstrated to have adopted an "anti-semitic" ideology.

Influences upon Hitler in Vienna

Hitler was genuinely influenced in Vienna by two political movements. The first was the German racist nationalism propagated by the Upper Austrian Pan-German politician, **Georg von Schönerer**. The second key influence was that of **Karl Lueger**, Mayor of Vienna from 1897 to his death in 1910.

Lueger was still in power when Hitler arrived in Vienna. Lueger promoted an anti-semitism that was more practical and organizational than ideological. Nevertheless, it reinforced anti-Jewish stereotypes and cast Jews as enemies of the German middle and lower classes. Unlike Schönerer, who was more comfortable with the elitist nationalism of the student fraternities, Lueger was comfortable with big city crowds and knew how to channel their protest into political gain. Hitler drew his ideology in large part from Schönerer, but his strategy and tactics from Lueger.

Munich

Hitler moved to Munich, Germany, in May 1913. He did so to avoid arrest for evading his military service obligation to Habsburg Austria. He financed his move with the last installment of his inheritance from his father. In Munich, he continued to drift. He supported himself on his watercolors and sketches until the outbreak of World War I gave his life direction and a cause to which he could commit himself totally.

He also developed an admiration for **Martin Luther**. Hitler read local newspapers such as Deutsches Volksblatt [de] that fanned prejudice and played on Christian fears of being swamped by an influx of Eastern European Jews. He read newspapers and pamphlets that published the thoughts of philosophers and theoreticians such as **Houston Stewart Chamberlain, Charles Darwin, Friedrich Nietzsche, Gustave Le Bon** and **Arthur Schopenhauer.**

The origin and development of Hitler's anti-Semitism remains a matter of debate. His friend, **August Kubizek** claimed that Hitler was a "confirmed anti-Semite" before he left Linz. However, historian **Brigitte Hamann** describes Kubizek's claim as "problematical". While Hitler states in **'Mein Kampf'** that he first became an anti-Semite in Vienna, Reinhold Hanisch, who helped him sell his paintings, disagrees. Hitler had dealings with Jews while living in Vienna. Historian Richard J. Evans states that "historians now generally agree that his notorious, murderous anti-Semitism emerged well after Germany's defeat [in World War I], as a product of the paranoid "stab-in-the-back" explanation for the catastrophe".

Hitler received the final part of his father's estate in May 1913 and moved to Munich, Germany. When he was conscripted into the Austro-Hungarian Army, he journeyed to Salzburg on 5th February 1914 for medical assessment. After he was deemed unfit for service, he returned to Munich. Hitler later claimed that he did not wish to serve the Habsburg Empire because of the mixture of races in its army and his belief that the collapse of Austria-Hungary was imminent.

Chapter - 2

Military Career of Adolf Hitler

In 1913, Hitler moved to Munich, in the German state of Bavaria. When World War I broke out in August 1914 , he successfully petitioned the Bavarian king to be allowed to volunteer in a reserve infantry regiment.

According to a 1924 report by the Bavarian authorities, allowing Hitler to serve was almost certainly an administrative error, since as an Austrian citizen, he should have been returned to Austria. Posted to the **Bavarian Reserve Infantry Regiment 16** (1st Company of the List Regiment), he served as a dispatch runner on the Western Front in France and Belgium, spending nearly half his time at the regimental headquarters in Fournes-en-Weppes, well behind the front lines. In 1914, he was present at the **First Battle of Ypres** and in that year won two decorations for bravery, including the rare **Iron Cross, First Class** which he wore till the end of his life.

During his service at headquarters, Hitler pursued his artwork, drawing cartoons and instructions for an army newspaper. During the **Battle of Somme** in October 1916, he was wounded in the left thigh when a shell exploded in the dispatch runners' dugout. Hitler spent almost two months recovering in hospital at Beelitz, returning to his regiment on 5th March 1917. He was present at the **Battle of Arras** of 1917 and the **Battle of Passchendaele**. He received the **Black Wound Badge** on 18th May 1918 and in August 1918, on the recommendation by Lieutenant Hugo Gutmann, his Jewish superior, Hitler received the Iron Cross, First Class, a decoration rarely awarded to one of Hitler's Gefreiter rank. On 15th October 1918, he was temporarily blinded in a mustard gas attack and was hospitalised in Pasewalk. There, Hitler heard of Germany's defeat, and upon receiving this news, suffered a second bout of blindness.

Hitler described the war as "the greatest of all experiences", and was praised by his commanding officers for his bravery. His wartime experience reinforced his German patriotism, and he was shocked by Germany's capitulation in November 1918. His bitterness over the collapse of the war effort began to shape his ideology. Like other German nationalists, he believed the **Dolchstoßlegende** (stab-in-the-back myth), which claimed that the German army, "undefeated in the field" had been "stabbed in the back" on the home front by civilian leaders, Jews, Marxists and those who signed the armistice that ended the fighting—later dubbed the "November criminals."

The **Treaty of Versailles** stipulated that Germany had to relinquish several of its territories and de-militarise the Rhineland. The treaty imposed economic sanctions and levied heavy reparations on the country. Many Germans saw the treaty as an unjust humiliation. They especially objected to Article 231, which they interpreted as declaring Germany responsible for the war. The Versailles treaty and the economic, social, and political conditions in Germany after the war were later exploited by Hitler for political gain.

Entry into Politics

After World War I, Hitler returned to Munich. Without formal education or career prospects, he remained in the army. In July 1919 he was appointed **Verbindungsmann** (intelligence agent) of an Aufklärungskommando (reconnaissance unit) of the Reichswehr, assigned to influence other soldiers and to infiltrate the **German Workers' Party (DAP)**. At a DAP meeting on 12th September 1919, Party Chairman, Anton Drexler was impressed with Hitler's oratorical skills. He gave him a copy of his pamphlet **My Political Awakening**, which contained anti-Semitic, nationalist, anti-capitalist and anti-Marxist ideas. On the orders of his army superiors, Hitler applied to join the party, and within a week was accepted as party member 555 (the party began counting membership at 500 to give the impression they were a much larger party).

Hitler made his earliest known written statement about the Jewish question in a 16th September 1919 letter to Adolf Gemlich (now known as the **Gemlich** letter). In the letter, Hitler argues that the aim of the government "must unshakably be the removal of the Jews altogether."

At the DAP, Hitler met Dietrich Eckart, one of the party's founders and a member of the occult Thule Society. Eckart became Hitler's mentor, exchanging ideas with him and introducing him to a wide range of Munich society. To increase its appeal, the DAP changed its name to the **Nationalsozialistische Deutsche Arbeiterpartei (National Socialist German Workers' Party (NSDAP),** known colloquially as the **"Nazi Party")**. Hitler designed the party's banner of a swastika in a white circle on a red background.

Hitler was discharged from the army on 31st March 1920 and began working full-time for the party. The party's headquarter was in Munich, a hotbed of anti-government German nationalists determined to crush Marxism and undermine the Weimar Republic. In February 1921, he spoke to a crowd of over 6,000. To publicise the meeting, two truckloads of party supporters drove around Munich waving swastika flags and distributing leaflets. Hitler soon gained notoriety for his rowdy polemic speeches against the Treaty of Versailles, rival politicians, and especially against Marxists and Jews.

In June 1921, while Hitler and Eckart were on a fundraising trip to Berlin, a mutiny broke out within the Nazi Party in Munich. Members of its executive committee wanted to merge with the Nuremberg-based German Socialist Party (DSP). Hitler returned to Munich on 11th July and angrily tendered his resignation. The committee members realised that the resignation of their leading public figure and speaker would mean the end of the party. Hitler announced he would rejoin on the condition that he would replace Drexler as party chairman, and that the party headquarters would remain in Munich. The committee agreed, and he rejoined the party on 26th July as member 3,680. Hitler continued to face some opposition within the Nazi Party. Opponents of Hitler in the leadership had Hermann Esser expelled from the party, and they printed 3,000 copies of a pamphlet attacking Hitler as a traitor to the party. In the following days, Hitler spoke to several packed houses and defended himself and Esser, to thunderous applause. His strategy proved successful, and at a special party congress on 29th July, he was granted absolute powers as party chairman, replacing Drexler, by a vote of 533 to 1.

Hitler's vitriolic beer hall speeches began attracting regular audiences. A demagogue, he became adept at using populist themes, including the use of scapegoats, who were blamed for his listeners' economic hardships. Hitler used personal magnetism and an understanding of crowd psychology to his advantage while engaged in public speaking. Historians have noted the hypnotic effect of his rhetoric on large audiences, and of his eyes in small groups. Alfons Heck, a former member of the Hitler Youth, recalled:

"We erupted into a frenzy of nationalistic pride that bordered on hysteria. For minutes on end, we shouted at the top of our lungs, with tears streaming down our faces: Sieg Heil, Sieg Heil, Sieg Heil! From that moment on, I belonged to Adolf Hitler body and soul."

The early followers included Rudolf Hess, former air force ace Hermann Göring, and army captain Ernst Röhm. Röhm became head of the Nazis' paramilitary organisation, the **Sturmabteilung** (SA, "Stormtroopers"), which protected meetings and attacked political opponents. A critical influence on Hitler's thinking during this period was the Aufbau Vereinigung, a conspiratorial group of White Russian exiles and early Nazis. The group, financed with funds channelled from wealthy industrialists, introduced Hitler to the idea of a Jewish conspiracy, linking international finance with Bolshevism.

The programme of the Nazi Party was laid out in their 25-point programme on 24th February 1920. This did not represent a coherent ideology, but was a conglomeration of received ideas which had currency in the **völkisch Pan-Germanic movement,** such as ultranationalism, opposition to the Treaty of Versailles, distrust of capitalism, as well as some socialist ideas. For Hitler, though, the most important aspect of it was its strong anti-Semitic stance. He also perceived the programme as primarily a basis for propaganda and for attracting people to the party.

Beer Hall Putsch and Landsberg Prison

In 1923, Hitler enlisted the help of World War I General Erich Ludendorff for an attempted coup known as the **"Beer Hall Putsch"**. The Nazi Party used Italian Fascism as a model for their appearance and policies. Hitler wanted to emulate Benito Mussolini's **"March on Rome"** of 1922 by staging his own coup in Bavaria, to be followed by a challenge to the government in Berlin. Hitler and Ludendorff sought the support of Staatskommissar (State Commissioner) **Gustav Ritter von Kahr**, Bavaria's de facto ruler. However, Kahr, along with Police Chief Hans Ritter von Seisser and Reichswehr General Otto von Lossow, wanted to install a nationalist dictatorship without Hitler.

On 8th November 1923, Hitler and the SA stormed a public meeting of 3,000 people organised by Kahr in the Bürgerbräukeller, a beer hall in Munich. Interrupting Kahr's speech, he announced that the national revolution had begun and declared the formation of a new government with Ludendorff. Retiring to a back room, Hitler, with handgun drawn, demanded and got the support of Kahr, Seisser and Lossow. Hitler's forces initially succeeded in occupying the local Reichswehr and police headquarters, but Kahr and his cohorts quickly withdrew their support. Neither the army, nor the state police, joined forces with Hitler. The next day, Hitler and his followers marched from the beer hall to the Bavarian War Ministry to overthrow the Bavarian government, but police dispersed them. Sixteen Nazi Party members and four police officers were killed in the failed coup.

Hitler fled to the home of Ernst Hanfstaengl and by some accounts contemplated suicide. He was depressed but calm when arrested on 11th November 1923 for high treason. His trial before the special People's Court in Munich began in February 1924, and Alfred Rosenberg became temporary leader of the Nazi Party. On 1st April, Hitler was sentenced to five years' imprisonment at **Landsberg Prison**. There, he received friendly treatment from the guards, and was allowed mail from supporters and regular visits by party comrades. Pardoned by the Bavarian Supreme Court, he was released from jail on 20th December 1924, against the state prosecutor's objections. Including time on remand, Hitler served just over one year in prison.

While at Landsberg, Hitler dictated most of the first volume of **'Mein Kampf'** (My Struggle; originally entitled Four and a Half Years of Struggle against Lies, Stupidity, and Cowardice) at first to his chauffeur, Emil Maurice, and then to his deputy, Rudolf Hess. The book, dedicated to Thule Society member Dietrich Eckart, was an autobiography and exposition of his ideology. The book laid out Hitler's plans for transforming German society into one based on race. Throughout the book, Jews are equated with "germs" and presented as the "international poisoners" of society. According to Hitler's ideology, the only solution was their extermination. While Hitler did not describe exactly how this was to be accomplished, his "inherent genocidal thrust is undeniable", according to Ian Kershaw.

Published in two volumes in 1925 and 1926, **'Mein Kampf'** sold 228,000 copies between 1925 and 1932. One million copies were sold in 1933, Hitler's first year in office.

Shortly before Hitler was eligible for parole, the Bavarian government attempted to have him deported to Austria. The Austrian federal chancellor rejected the request on the specious grounds that his service in the German Army made his Austrian citizenship void. In response, Hitler formally renounced his Austrian citizenship on 7th April 1925.

Rebuilding the Nazi Party

At the time of Hitler's release from prison, politics in Germany had become less combative and the economy had improved, limiting Hitler's opportunities for political agitation. As a result of the failed Beer Hall Putsch, the Nazi Party and its affiliated organisations were banned in Bavaria. In a meeting with the Prime Minister of Bavaria Heinrich held on 4th January 1925, Hitler agreed to respect the state's authority and promised that he would seek political power only through the democratic process. The meeting paved the way for the ban on the Nazi Party to be lifted on 16th February. However, after an inflammatory speech he gave on 27th February, Hitler was barred from public speaking by the Bavarian authorities, a ban that remained in place until 1927. To advance his political ambitions in spite of the ban, Hitler appointed Gregor Strasser, Otto Strasser and Joseph Goebbels to organise and enlarge the Nazi Party in northern Germany. Gregor Strasser steered a more independent political course, emphasising the socialist elements of the party's programme.

The stock market in the United States crashed on 24th October 1929. The impact in Germany was dire: millions were thrown out of work and several major banks collapsed. Hitler and the Nazi Party prepared to take advantage of the emergency to gain support for their party. They promised to repudiate the Versailles Treaty, strengthen the economy, and provide jobs.

Chapter - 3

Adolf Hitler's Rise to Power

Adolf Hitler's rise to power began in the newly established Weimar Republic in September 1919 when Hitler joined the **Deutsche Arbeiterpartei (DAP; German Workers' Party)**. He rose to a place of prominence in the early years of the party. Being one of its best speakers, he was made the party leader after he threatened to leave.

In 1920, the DAP renamed itself to the **Nationalsozialistische Deutsche Arbeiterpartei – NSDAP** (National Socialist German Workers' Party, commonly known as the Nazi Party). Hitler chose this name to win over German workers. Despite the NSDAP being a right-wing party, it had many anti-capitalist and anti-bourgeois elements. Hitler later initiated a purge of these elements and reaffirmed the Nazi Party's pro-business stance. By 1922 Hitler's control over the party was unchallenged. In 1923, Hitler and his supporters attempted a coup in Bavaria. This seminal event was later called the **Beer Hall Putsch**. Upon its failure, Hitler escaped, only to be subsequently arrested and put on trial. The trial proved to be a blessing in disguise for Hitler, as it garnered him national fame. Hitler was sentenced to five years in prison, but he only served eight months. Once released, Hitler switched tactics; he was going to seize power through legal and democratic means.

Hitler, armed with his newfound celebrity, began furiously campaigning. During the 1920s, Hitler and the Nazis ran on a platform consisting of anti-communism, anti-semitism, and ultranationalism. Nazi party leaders vociferously criticized the ruling democratic government and the Treaty of Versailles, while proselytizing their desire to turn Germany into a world power. At this time, most Germans were indifferent to Hitler's rhetoric as the German economy was beginning to recover in large part due to loans from the United States under the **Dawes Plan**. The German political landscape was dramatically affected by the 1929 **Wall Street Crash,** which hampered economic aid to Germany. **The Great Depression** brought the German economy to a halt and further polarized German politics. Hitler and the Nazis began to exploit the crisis and loudly criticized the ruling government. During this tumultuous time, the German Communist Party also began campaigning and called for a revolution. Business leaders, fearful of a communist takeover, began supporting the Nazi party. In 1932, the Nazis held the largest number of seats in the Reichstag, albeit short of an absolute majority. Seeking to capture the rising Nazi electoral success, Hitler ran for the presidency in 1932 but was defeated by the incumbent **Paul von Hindenburg.**

1933 was a pivotal year for Hitler and the Nazi Party. Traditionally, the leader of the party who held the most seats in the Reichstag was appointed Chancellor. However, President Paul von Hindenburg was hesitant to appoint Hitler as chancellor. Following several backroom negotiations – which included industrialists, Hindenburg's son, the former chancellor Franz von Papen, and Hitler – Hindenburg acquiesced and on 30th January 1933, he formally appointed Adolf Hitler as Germany's new chancellor. Although he was chancellor, Hitler was not yet an absolute dictator.

The groundwork for the Nazi dictatorship was laid when the Reichstag was set on fire in February. Believing the communists were behind the arson, Hitler convinced Paul von Hindenburg to pass the **Reichstag Fire Decree**, which severely curtailed the liberties and rights of German citizens. Using the decree, Hitler began eliminating his political opponents. In Hitler's eyes the decree was insufficient and he proposed **the Enabling Act of 1933.** This law gave the German government the power to override individual rights prescribed by the constitution. The law also gave the

Chancellor (Hitler) emergency powers to pass and enforce laws without parliamentary oversight. The Enabling Act was passed in March and by April, Hitler held de facto dictatorial powers and used them to order the construction of the first **Nazi concentration camp at Dachau** for communists and other political opponents. Hitler's rise to power was completed in August 1934 when President Paul von Hindenburg died. Hitler merged the Chancellorship with the Presidency and became the **Führer** of Germany.

In retrospect, Hitler's rise to power was aided in part by his willingness to use violence in advancing his political objectives and to recruit party members willing to do the same. Furthermore, Hitler went out of his way to seek financial support from wealthy businessmen, without whose support his assumption of power would have been impossible. Hitler framed their partnership as an essential factor in defeating the rising threat of communism. The party engaged in electoral battles in which Hitler participated as a speaker and organizer. Street battles and violence also erupted between the **Communists' Rotfrontkämpferbund** and the **Nazis' Sturmabteilung (SA).**

Once the Nazi dictatorship was firmly established, the Nazis themselves created a mythology surrounding their rise to power. German propaganda described this time period as either the Kampfzeit (the time of struggle) or the Kampfjahre (years of struggle).

Early Germany

Historians have commented on the influence of German Chancellor Otto von Bismarck's process of "negative integration" as setting a tone of exclusion in early Germany, which had a lasting influence on later German nationalism. Bismarck sought to prevent the religious and political divisions in early Germany by rallying the populace against a common enemy. Initially Bismarck ran a campaign against the Catholic church from 1873 to the late 1870s, referred to as **Kulturkampf**, questioning whether they were loyal to Berlin or other Catholic states. Instead of uniting German people, it instead resulted in a bolstering of support to the Catholic church, alienating an important religious minority. In 1878, Bismarck then introduced a number of anti-socialist laws that would be in effect from 1878-1890 in an attempt to alienate the Social Democratic Party. While some sections of German society were united by this, many industrial workers rallied to the SDP. Historians have expressed that as the German state was still very new at the time, it was therefore impressionable; Bismarck's strategy of confrontation rather than consensus set a tone of either being loyal to the government or an enemy of the state, which directly influenced German nationalist sentiment and the later Nazi movement.

Early Steps (1918–1924)

Adolf Hitler became involved with the fledgling **German Workers' Party** – which he would later transform into the Nazi Party – after the First World War, and set the violent tone of the movement early, by forming the **Sturmabteilung (SA)** paramilitary. Catholic Bavaria resented rule from Protestant Berlin, and Hitler at first saw revolution in Bavaria as a means to power. An early attempt at a coup d'état, the 1923 Beer Hall Putsch in Munich, proved fruitless, however, and Hitler was imprisoned for leading the putsch. He used this time to write **'Mein Kampf'** in which he argued that effeminate Jewish–Christian ethics were enfeebling Europe, and that Germany was in need of an uncompromising strongman to restore itself and build an empire. Learning from the failed coup, he decided on the tactic of pursuing power through legal means rather than seizing control of the government by force against the state and instead proclaimed a strictly legal course.

From Armistice (November 1918) to party membership (September 1919)

In 1914, after being granted permission from King Ludwig III of Bavaria, the 25-year-old Austrian-born Hitler enlisted in a Bavarian regiment of the German Army, although he was not yet a German citizen. For over four years (August 1914 – November 1918), Germany was a major participant in World War I. After fighting on the Western Front ended in November 1918, Hitler was discharged on 19th November from the Pasewalk hospital and returned to Munich, which at the time was in a state of socialist upheaval. Arriving on 21st November, he was assigned to 7th Company of the 1st Replacement Battalion of the 2nd Infantry Regiment. In December, he was reassigned to a prisoner-of-war camp in Traunstein as a guard. He remained there until the camp dissolved in January 1919, after which he returned to Munich and spent a couple weeks on guard duty at the city's main train station (Hauptbahnhof) through which soldiers had been traveling.

During this time a number of notable Germans were assassinated, including socialist Kurt Eisner, who was shot dead by a German nationalist on 21st February 1919. His rival Erhard Auer was also wounded in an attack. Other acts of violence were the killings of both Major Paul Ritter von Jahreiß and the conservative MP Heinrich Osel. In this political chaos Berlin sent in the military – called the **"White Guards of Capitalism"** by the communists. On 3rd April 1919, Hitler was elected as the liaison of his military battalion and again on 15th April. During this time he urged his unit to stay out of the fighting and not to join either side.

The Bavarian Soviet Republic was officially crushed on 6th May, when Lieutenant General Burghard von Oven and his forces declared the city secure. In the aftermath of arrests and executions, Hitler denounced a fellow liaison, Georg Dufter, as a Soviet "radical rabble-rouser." Other testimony he gave to the military board of inquiry allowed them to root out other members of the military that "had been infected with revolutionary fervor." For his anti-communist views he was allowed to avoid discharge when his unit was disbanded in May 1919.

In June 1919, Hitler was moved to the demobilization office of the 2nd Infantry Regiment. Around this time the German military command released an edict that the army's main priority was to "carry out, in conjunction with the police, stricter surveillance of the population ... so that the ignition of any new unrest can be discovered and extinguished." In May 1919, Karl Mayr became commander of the 6th Battalion of the guards regiment in Munich and from 30th May the head of the "Education and Propaganda Department" of the General Command von Oven and the Group Command No. 4 (Department Ib). In this capacity as head of the intelligence department, Mayr recruited Hitler as an undercover agent in early June 1919. Under Captain Mayr, "national thinking" courses were arranged at the Reichswehrlager Lechfeld near Augsburg, with Hitler attending from 10th to 19th July. During this time Hitler so impressed Mayr that he assigned him to an anti-Bolshevik "educational commando" as 1 of 26 instructors in the summer of 1919.

In July 1919, Hitler was appointed **Verbindungsmann** (intelligence agent) of an Aufklärungskommando (reconnaissance commando) of the Reichswehr, both to influence other soldiers and to infiltrate the German Workers' Party (DAP). The DAP had been formed by Anton Drexler, Karl Harrer and others, through amalgamation of other groups, on 5th January 1919 at a small gathering at the restaurant Fuerstenfelder Hof in Munich.

 THE RISE OF ADOLF HITLER

While he studied the activities of the DAP, Hitler became impressed with Drexler's antisemitic, nationalist, anti-capitalist and anti-Marxist ideas.

During the 12th September 1919 meeting, Hitler took umbrage with comments made by an audience member that were directed against Gottfried Feder, the speaker, a crank economist with whom Hitler was acquainted due to a lecture Feder delivered in an army "education" course. The audience member asserted that Bavaria should be wholly independent from Germany and should secede from Germany and unite with Austria to form a new south German nation. The volatile Hitler arose and scolded the man, eventually causing him to leave the meeting before its adjournment.

Impressed with Hitler's oratory skills, Drexler encouraged him to join the DAP. On the orders of his army superiors, Hitler applied to join the party. Within a week, Hitler received a postcard stating he had officially been accepted as a member and he should come to a "committee" meeting to discuss it. Hitler attended the "committee" meeting held at the run-down Alte Rosenbad beer-house. Later Hitler wrote that joining the fledgling party "...was the most decisive resolve of my life. From here there was and could be no turning back. ... I registered as a member of the German Workers' Party and received a provisional membership card with the number 7". Normally, enlisted army personnel were not allowed to join political parties. However, in this case, Hitler had Captain Mayr's permission to join the DAP. Further, Hitler was allowed to stay in the army and receive his weekly pay of 20 gold marks.

From early party membership to the Hofbräuhaus Melée (November 1921)

By early 1920, the DAP had grown to over 101 members, and Hitler received his membership card as member number 555 (the numbers started from 501). Hitler's considerable oratory and propaganda skills were appreciated by the party leadership. With the support of Anton Drexler, Hitler became chief of propaganda for the party in early 1920 and his actions began to transform the party. He organised their biggest meeting yet, of 2,000 people, on 24th February 1920 in the Staatliches Hofbräuhaus in München. There Hitler announced the party's 25-point program (see National Socialist Program). He also engineered the name change of the DAP to the **Nationalsozialistische Deutsche Arbeiterpartei** – NSDAP (National Socialist German Workers' Party), later known to the rest of the world as the **Nazi Party.** Hitler designed the party's banner of a swastika in a white circle on a red background. He was discharged from the army in March 1920 and began working full-time for the Nazi Party.

In 1920, a small "hall protection" squad was organised around Emil Maurice. The group was first named the **"Order troops"** (Ordnertruppen). Later in August 1921, Hitler redefined the group, which became known as the "Gymnastic and Sports Division" of the party (Turn- und Sportabteilung). By the autumn of 1921 the group was being called the **Sturmabteilung ("Storm Detachment")** or SA, and by November 1921 the group was officially known by that name. Also in 1920, Hitler began to lecture in Munich beer halls, particularly the Hofbräuhaus, Sterneckerbräu and Bürgerbräukeller. Only Hitler was able to bring in the crowds for the party speeches and meetings. By this time, the police were already monitoring the speeches, and their own surviving records reveal that Hitler delivered lectures with titles such as Political Phenomenon, Jews and the Treaty of Versailles. At the end of the year, party membership was recorded at 2,000.

In June 1921, while Hitler and Dietrich Eckart were on a fundraising trip to Berlin, a mutiny broke out within the Nazi Party in Munich, its organizational home. Members of its executive committee wanted to merge with the rival German Socialist Party (DSP). Hitler returned to Munich on 11th July and angrily tendered his resignation. The committee members realised that the resignation of their leading public figure and speaker would mean the end of the party. Hitler announced he would rejoin on the condition that he would replace Drexler as party chairman and that the party headquarters would remain in Munich. The committee agreed, and he rejoined the party on 26th July as member 3,680. In the following days, Hitler spoke to several packed houses and defended himself, to thunderous applause. His strategy proved successful: at a general membership meeting, he was granted absolute powers as party chairman, with only one nay vote cast.

On 14th September 1921, Hitler and a substantial number of SA members and other Nazi Party adherents disrupted a meeting of the Bavarian League at the Löwenbräukeller. This federalist organization objected to the centralism of the Weimar Constitution but accepted its social program. The League was led by Otto Ballerstedt, an engineer whom Hitler regarded as "my most dangerous opponent". One Nazi, Hermann Esser, climbed upon a chair and shouted that the Jews were to blame for the misfortunes of Bavaria and the Nazis shouted demands

 THE RISE OF ADOLF HITLER

that Ballerstedt yield the floor to Hitler. The Nazis beat up Ballerstedt and shoved him off the stage into the audience. Hitler and Esser were arrested and Hitler commented notoriously to the police commissioner, "It's all right. We got what we wanted. Ballerstedt did not speak".

Less than two months later, on 4th November 1921, the Nazi Party held a large public meeting in the Munich Hofbräuhaus. After Hitler had spoken for some time, the meeting erupted into a melée in which a small company of SA defeated the opposition. For his part in these events, Hitler was eventually sentenced in January 1922 to three months' imprisonment for "breach of the peace", but only spent a little over one month at Stadelheim Prison in Munich.

From Beer Hall melée to Beer Hall coup d'état

In 1922 and early 1923, Hitler and the Nazi Party formed two organizations that would grow to have huge significance. The first began as the **Jungsturm Adolf Hitler** and the **Jugendbund der NSDAP**; they would later become the Hitler Youth. The other was the **Stabswache (Staff Guard)**, which in May 1923 was renamed the Stoßtrupp-Hitler (Shock Troop-Hitler). This early incarnation of a bodyguard unit for Hitler would later become the Schutzstaffel (SS). Inspired by Benito Mussolini's March on Rome in 1922, Hitler decided that a coup d'état was the proper strategy to seize control of the German government. In May 1923, small elements loyal to Hitler within the Reichswehr helped the SA to illegally procure a barracks and its weaponry, but the order to march never came, possibly because Hitler had been warned by Army General Otto von Lossow that "he would be fired upon" by Reichswehr troops if they attempted a putsch.

A pivotal moment came when Hitler led the Beer Hall Putsch, an attempted coup d'état on 8–9 November 1923. At the Bürgerbräukeller in Munich, Hitler and his deputies announced their plan: Bavarian government officials would be deposed and Hitler installed at the head of government, with Munich then used as a base camp from which to march on Berlin. Nearly 2,000 Nazi Party members proceeded to the Marienplatz in Munich's city center, where they were met by a police cordon summoned to obstruct them. Sixteen Nazi Party members and four police officers were killed in the ensuing violence. Hitler briefly escaped the city but was arrested on 11th November 1923, and put on trial for high treason, which gained him widespread public attention.

The trial began in February 1924. Hitler endeavored to turn the tables and put democracy and the Weimar Republic on trial as traitors to the German people. Hitler was convicted and on 1st April sentenced to five years' imprisonment at Landsberg Prison. He received friendly treatment from the guards; he had a room with a view of the river, wore a tie, had regular visitors to his chambers, was allowed mail from supporters and was permitted the use of a private secretary. Pardoned by the Bavarian Supreme Court, he was released from jail on 20th December 1924, after serving just nine months, against the state prosecutor's objections.

Hitler used the time in Landsberg Prison to reconsider his political strategy and dictate the first volume of **Mein Kampf** (My Struggle; originally entitled Four and a Half Years of Struggle against Lies, Stupidity, and Cowardice), principally to his deputy Rudolf Hess. After the Beer Hall Putsch, the Nazi Party was banned in Bavaria, but it participated in 1924's two elections by proxy as the National Socialist Freedom Movement. In the May 1924 German federal election the party gained seats in the Reichstag, with 6.6% (1,918,329) voting for the Movement. In the December 1924 federal election, the National Socialist Freedom Movement (NSFB) (combination of the Deutschvölkische Freiheitspartei (DVFP) and the Nazi Party (NSDAP)) lost 18 seats, only holding on to 14 seats, with 3% (907,242) of the electorate voting for Hitler's party. The Barmat Scandal was often used later in Nazi propaganda, both as an electoral strategy and as an appeal to anti-Semitism.

After some reflection, Hitler had determined that power was to be achieved not through revolution outside of the government, but rather through what he called "the path of legality" within the confines of the democratic system established by Weimar. For five to six years, there would be no further prohibitions of the party.

Move towards power (1925–1930)

In the May 1928 federal election, the Nazi Party achieved just 12 seats in the Reichstag. The highest provincial gain was again in Bavaria (5.1%), though in three areas the Nazis failed to gain even 1% of the vote. Overall, the party gained 2.6% of the vote (810,100 votes). Partially due to the poor results, Hitler decided that Germans needed to know more about his goals. Despite being discouraged by his publisher, he wrote a second book that was discovered and released posthumously as the Zweites Buch. At this time the SA began a period of deliberate antagonism to the Rotfront by marching into Communist strongholds and starting violent altercations.

At the end of 1928, party membership was recorded at 130,000. In March 1929, Erich Ludendorff represented the Nazi Party in the Presidential elections. He earned 280,000 votes (1.1%), and was the only candidate to poll fewer than a million votes. The battles on the streets grew increasingly violent. After the Rotfront interrupted a speech by Hitler, the SA marched into the streets of Nuremberg and killed two bystanders. In a tit-for-tat action, the SA stormed a Rotfront meeting on 25th August and days later the Berlin headquarters of the Communist Party of Germany (KPD) itself. In September, Goebbels led his men into Neukölln, a KPD stronghold, and the two warring parties exchanged pistol and revolver fire. The German referendum of 1929 was important as it gained the Nazi Party recognition and credibility it had never had before. In the late 1920s, seeing the party's lack of breakthrough into the mainstream, Goebbels proposed that instead of focusing all of their propaganda in major cities where there was competition from other political movements, they should instead begin holding rallies in rural areas where they would be more effective.

On the evening of 14th January 1930, at around ten o'clock, Horst Wessel was fatally shot in the face at point-blank range by two members of the KPD in Friedrichshain.[56] The attack occurred after an argument with his landlady, who was a member of the KPD and contacted one of her Rotfront friends, Albert Hochter, who shot Wessel. Wessel had penned a song months before which would become a Nazi anthem as the Horst-Wessel-Lied. Goebbels seized upon the attack (and the weeks Wessel spent on his deathbed) to publicize the song, and the funeral was used as an anti-Communist propaganda opportunity for the Nazis. In May, Goebbels was convicted of "libeling" President Hindenburg and fined 800 marks. The conviction stemmed from a 1929 article by Goebbels in his newspaper Der Angriff. In June, Goebbels was charged with high treason by the prosecutor in Leipzig based on statements Goebbels had made in 1927, but after a four-month investigation it came to naught.

Against this backdrop, Hitler's party gained a significant victory in the Reichstag, obtaining 107 seats (18.3%, 6,409,600 votes) in the September 1930 federal election. The Nazis thereby became the second-largest party in Germany, and as historian Joseph Bendersky notes, they essentially became the "dominant political force on the right".

An unprecedented amount of money was thrown behind the campaign and political success increased the party's momentum as it recorded over 100,000 new members in the next few months following the election.

Well over one million pamphlets were produced and distributed; sixty trucks were commandeered for use in Berlin alone. In areas where Nazi campaigning was less rigorous, the total share of the vote was as low as 9%. The **Great Depression** was also a factor in Hitler's electoral success. Against this legal backdrop, the SA began its first major anti-Jewish action on 13th October 1930, when groups of Nazi brownshirts smashed the windows of Jewish-owned stores at Potsdamer Platz.

Weimar parties fail to halt Nazis

The Wall Street Crash of 1929 heralded worldwide economic disaster. The Nazis and the Communists made great gains at the 1930 federal election. The Nazis and Communists between them secured almost 40% of Reichstag seats, which required the moderate parties to consider negotiations with anti-democrats. "The Communists", wrote historian Alan Bullock, "openly announced that they would prefer to see the Nazis in power rather than lift a finger to save the republic".

The Weimar political parties failed to stop the Nazi rise. Germany's Weimar political system made it difficult for chancellors to govern with a stable parliamentary majority, and successive chancellors instead relied on the president's emergency powers to govern. In 1931 the Nazi Party altered its strategy to engage in perpetual campaigning across the country, even outside of election time. From 1931 to 1933, the Nazis combined terror tactics with conventional campaigning – Hitler criss-crossed the nation by air, while SA troops paraded in the streets, beat up opponents, and broke up their meetings. Systematic statistical analyses demonstrate that voters responded the way they do in most modern elections, which explains why certain identifiable groups turned to the Nazis and others turned away.

A middle-class liberal party strong enough to block the Nazis did not exist – the People's Party and the Democrats suffered severe losses to the Nazis at the polls. The Social Democrats were essentially a conservative trade union party, with ineffectual leadership. The Catholic Centre Party maintained its voting block, but was preoccupied with defending its own particular interests and, wrote Bullock: "through 1932–3 ... was so far from recognizing the danger of a Nazi dictatorship that it continued to negotiate with the Nazis". The Communists meanwhile were engaging in violent clashes with Nazis on the streets, but Moscow had directed the Communist Party to prioritise destruction of the Social Democrats, seeing more danger in them as a rival for the loyalty of the working class. Nevertheless, wrote

 THE RISE OF ADOLF HITLER

Bullock, the heaviest responsibility lay with the German right wing, who "forsook a true conservatism" and made Hitler their partner in a coalition government.

The Centre Party's Heinrich Brüning was Chancellor from 1930 to 1932. Brüning and Hitler were unable to reach terms of co-operation, but Brüning himself increasingly governed with the support of the President and Army over that of the parliament. The 84-year-old President von Hindenburg, a conservative monarchist, was reluctant to take action to suppress the Nazis, while the ambitious Major-General Kurt von Schleicher, as Minister handling army and navy matters hoped to harness their support. With Schleicher's backing, and Hitler's stated approval, Hindenburg appointed the Catholic monarchist Franz von Papen to replace Brüning as Chancellor in June 1932. Papen had been active in the resurgence of the Harzburg Front. He had fallen out with the Centre Party. He hoped ultimately to outmaneuver Hitler.

At the July 1932 federal election, the Nazis became the largest party in the Reichstag, yet without a majority. Hitler withdrew support for Papen and demanded the Chancellorship. He was refused by Hindenburg. Papen dissolved Parliament, and the Nazi vote declined at the November election. In the aftermath of the election, Papen proposed ruling by decree while drafting a new electoral system, with an upper house. Schleicher convinced Hindenburg to sack Papen, and Schleicher himself became Chancellor, promising to form a workable coalition.

The aggrieved Papen opened negotiations with Hitler, proposing a Nazi-Nationalist Coalition. Having nearly outmaneuvered Hitler, only to be trounced by Schleicher, Papen turned his attentions on defeating Schleicher, and concluded an agreement with Hitler.

Seizure of control (1931–1933)

On 10th March 1931, with street violence between the Rotfront and SA increasing, breaking all previous barriers and expectations, Prussia re-enacted its ban on Brownshirts. Days after the ban, SA-men shot dead two communists in a street fight, which led to a ban being placed on the public speaking of Goebbels, who sidestepped the prohibition by recording speeches and playing them to an audience in his absence.

When Hitler's citizenship became a matter of public discussion in 1924 he had a public declaration printed on 16th October 1924,

"The loss of my Austrian citizenship is not painful to me, as I never felt as an Austrian citizen but always as a German only. ... It was this mentality that made me draw the ultimate conclusion and do military service in the German Army."

Under the threat of criminal deportation home to Austria, Hitler formally renounced his Austrian citizenship on 7th April 1925, and did not acquire German citizenship until almost seven years later; therefore, he was unable to run for public office. Hitler gained German citizenship after being appointed a Free State of Brunswick government official by Dietrich Klagges, after an earlier attempt by Wilhelm Frick to convey citizenship as a Thuringian police official failed.

Ernst Röhm, in charge of the SA, put Wolf-Heinrich von Helldorff, a vehement anti-Semite, in charge of the Berlin SA. The deaths mounted, with many more on the Rotfront side, and by the end of 1931 the SA had suffered 47 deaths and the Rotfront recorded losses of approximately 80 killed. Street fights and beer hall battles resulting in deaths occurred throughout February and April 1932, all against the backdrop of Adolf Hitler's competition in the presidential election which pitted him against the monumentally popular Hindenburg. In the first round on 13th March, Hitler had polled over 11 million votes but was still behind Hindenburg. The second and final round took place on 10th April: Hitler (36.8% 13,418,547) lost to Paul von Hindenburg (53.0% 19,359,983) while the KPD candidate Thälmann gained a meagre percentage of the vote (10.2% 3,706,759). At this time, the Nazi Party had just over 800,000 members.

On 13th April 1932, following the presidential elections, the German government banned the Nazi Party paramilitaries, the SA and the SS, on the basis of the Emergency Decree for the Preservation of State Authority. This action was prompted by details uncovered by the Prussian police that indicated the SA was ready for a takeover of power by force after an election of Hitler. The lifting of the ban and staging of new elections were the price Hitler demanded in exchange for his support of a new cabinet. The law was repealed on 16 June by Franz von Papen, Chancellor of Germany as part of his agreement with Hitler. In the federal election of July 1932, the Nazis won 37.3% of the popular vote (13,745,000 votes), an upswing by 19 percent, becoming the largest party in the Reichstag, with 230 out of 608 seats. Dwarfed by Hitler's electoral gains, the KPD turned away from legal means and increasingly towards violence. One resulting battle in Silesia resulted in the army being dispatched, each shot sending Germany further into a potential civil war. By this time both sides marched into each other's strongholds hoping to spark a rivalry. The attacks continued and reached fever pitch when SA leader Axel Schaffeld was assassinated on 1st August.

As the Nazi Party was now the largest party in the Reichstag, it was entitled to select the President of the Reichstag and were able to elect Göring for the post. Energised by the success, Hitler asked to be made chancellor. Hitler was offered the job of vice-chancellor by Chancellor Papen at the behest of President Hindenburg but he refused. Hitler saw this offer as placing him in a position of "playing second fiddle" in the government.

In his position of Reichstag president, Göring asked that decisive measures be taken by the government over the spate of murders of Nazi Party members. On 9th August, amendments were made to the Reichstrafgesetzbuch statute on "acts of political violence", increasing the penalty to "lifetime imprisonment, 20 years hard labour or death". Special courts were announced to try such offences. When in power less than half a year later, Hitler would use this legislation against his opponents with devastating effect.

The law was applied almost immediately but did not bring the perpetrators behind the recent massacres to trial as expected. Instead, five SA men who were alleged to have murdered a KPD member in Potempa (Upper Silesia) were tried. Hitler appeared at the trial as a defence witness, but on 22nd August the five were convicted and sentenced to death. On appeal, this sentence was commuted to life imprisonment in early September. They served just over four months before Hitler freed all imprisoned Nazis in a 1933 amnesty.

The Nazi Party lost 35 seats in the November 1932 election, but remained the Reichstag's largest party, with 196 seats (33.1%). The Social Democrats (SPD) won 121 seats (20.4%) and the Communists (KPD) won 100 (16.9%).

The Communist International described all moderate left-wing parties as "social fascists" and urged the Communists to devote their energies to the destruction of the moderate left. As a result, the KPD, following orders from Moscow, rejected overtures from the Social Democrats to form a political alliance against the NSDAP.

After Chancellor Papen left office, he secretly told Hitler that he still held considerable sway with President Hindenburg and that he would make Hitler chancellor as long as he, Papen, could be the vice chancellor.

Another notable event was the publication of the **Industrielleneingabe,** a letter signed by 22 important representatives of industry, finance and agriculture, asking Hindenburg to appoint Hitler as chancellor. Hindenburg reluctantly agreed to appoint Hitler as chancellor after the parliamentary elections of July and November 1932 had not resulted in the formation of a majority government – despite the fact that Hitler had been Hindenburg's opponent in the presidential election only 9 months earlier. Hitler headed a short-lived coalition government formed by the NSDAP and the German National People's Party (DNVP).

On 30th January 1933, the new cabinet was sworn in during a brief ceremony in Hindenburg's office. The NSDAP gained three posts: Hitler was named chancellor, Wilhelm Frick Minister of the Interior, and Hermann Göring, Minister Without Portfolio (and Minister of the Interior for Prussia). The SA and SS led torchlit parades throughout Berlin. It is this event that would become termed Hitler's **Machtergreifung** ("seizure of power"). The term was originally used by some Nazis to suggest a revolutionary process, though Hitler, and others, used the word **Machtübernahme** ("take-over of power"), reflecting that the transfer of power took place within the existing constitutional framework and suggesting that the process was legal.

Papen was to serve as Vice-Chancellor in a majority conservative Cabinet – still falsely believing that he could "tame" Hitler. Initially, Papen did speak out against some Nazi excesses. However, after narrowly escaping death in the **Night of the Long Knives** in 1934, he no longer dared criticise the regime and was sent off to Vienna as German ambassador.

Both within Germany and abroad, there were initially few fears that Hitler could use his position to establish his later dictatorial single-party regime. Rather, the conservatives that helped to make him chancellor were convinced that they could control Hitler and "tame" the Nazi Party while setting the relevant impulses in the government themselves; foreign ambassadors played down worries by emphasizing that Hitler was "mediocre" if not a bad copy of Mussolini; even SPD politician Kurt Schumacher trivialized Hitler as a Dekorationsstück ("piece of scenery/ decoration") of the new government. German newspapers wrote that, without doubt, the Hitler-led government would try to fight its political enemies (the left-wing parties), but that it would be impossible to establish a dictatorship in Germany because there was "a barrier, over which violence cannot proceed" and because of the German nation being proud of "the

     THE RISE OF ADOLF HITLER

freedom of speech and thought". Benno Reifenberg of the Frankfurter Zeitung wrote:

"It is a hopeless misjudgement to think that one could force a dictatorial regime upon the [German] nation. [...] The diversity of the German people calls for democracy." — **Benno Reifenberg**

However, a growing number of keen observers, like Sir Horace Rumbold, British Ambassador in Berlin, began to revise their opinions. On 22nd February 1933, he wrote, "Hitler may be no statesman but he is an uncommonly clever and audacious demagogue and fully alive to every popular instinct", and he informed the Foreign Office that he had no doubt that the Nazis had "come to stay".

On receiving the dispatch Robert Vansittart, Permanent Under-Secretary of State for Foreign Affairs, concluded that if Hitler eventually gained the upper hand, "then another European war [was] within measurable distance".

With Germans who opposed Nazism failing to unite against it, Hitler soon moved to consolidate absolute power.

"At the risk of appearing to talk nonsense I tell you that the National Socialist movement will go on for 1,000 years! ... Don't forget how people laughed at me 15 years ago when I declared that one day I would govern Germany. They laugh now, just as foolishly, when I declare that I shall remain in power!" —**Adolf Hitler to a British correspondent in Berlin, June 1934**

Chancellor to Dictator

Following the **Reichstag fire**, the Nazis began to suspend civil liberties and eliminate political opposition. The Communists were excluded from the Reichstag. At the March 1933 elections, again no single party secured a majority. Hitler required the vote of the Centre Party and Conservatives in the Reichstag to obtain the powers he desired. He called on Reichstag members to vote for the **Enabling Act** on 23rd March 1933. Hitler was granted plenary powers "temporarily" by the passage of the Act. The law gave him the freedom to act without parliamentary consent and even without constitutional limitations.

Employing his characteristic mix of negotiation and intimidation, Hitler offered the possibility of friendly co-operation, promising not to threaten the Reichstag, the President, the States or the Churches if granted the emergency powers. With Nazi paramilitary encircling the building, he said: "It is for you, gentlemen of the Reichstag to decide between war and peace". The Centre Party, having obtained promises of non-interference in religion, joined with conservatives in voting for the Act (only the Social Democrats voted against).

The Act allowed Hitler and his Cabinet to rule by emergency decree for four years, though Hindenburg remained President. Hitler immediately set about abolishing the powers of the states and the existence of non-Nazi political parties and organisations. Non-Nazi parties were formally outlawed on 14th July 1933, and the Reichstag abdicated its democratic responsibilities. Hindenburg remained commander-in-chief of the military and retained the power to negotiate foreign treaties.

The Act did not infringe upon the powers of the President, and Hitler would not fully achieve full dictatorial power until after the death of Hindenburg in August 1934. Journalists and diplomats wondered whether Hitler could appoint himself President, who might succeed him as Chancellor, and what the army would do. They did not know that the army supported Hitler after the Night of the Long Knives, or expect that he would combine the two positions of President and Chancellor into one office with the "Law Concerning the Head of State of the German Reich". Only Hitler, as head of state, could dismiss Hitler as head of the government. All soldiers took the **Hitler Oath** on the day of Hindenburg's death, swearing unconditional obedience to Hitler personally, not to the office or nation. A large majority approved of combining the two roles in the person of Hitler through the 1934 German referendum.

Chapter - 4

World War 1 contd...

Brüning Administration

The Great Depression provided a political opportunity for Hitler. Germans were ambivalent about the parliamentary republic, which faced challenges from right- and left-wing extremists. The moderate political parties were increasingly unable to stem the tide of extremism, and the German referendum of 1929 helped to elevate Nazi ideology. The elections of September 1930 resulted in the break-up of a grand coalition and its replacement with a minority cabinet. Its leader, chancellor, **Heinrich Brüning of the Centre Party**, governed through emergency decrees from President Paul von Hindenburg. Governance by decree became the new norm and paved the way for authoritarian forms of government. The Nazi Party rose from obscurity to win 18.3 per cent of the vote and 107 parliamentary seats in the 1930 election, becoming the second-largest party in parliament.

Hitler made a prominent appearance at the trial of two Reichswehr officers, **Lieutenants Richard Scheringer** and **Hanns Ludin**, in late 1930. Both were charged with membership in the Nazi Party, at that time illegal for Reichswehr personnel. The prosecution argued that the Nazi Party was an extremist party, prompting defence lawyer Hans Frank to call on Hitler to testify. On 25th September 1930, Hitler testified that his party would pursue political power solely through democratic elections, which won him many supporters in the officer corps.

Brüning's austerity measures brought little economic improvement and were extremely unpopular. Hitler exploited this by targeting his political messages specifically at people who had been affected by the inflation of the 1920s and the Depression, such as farmers, war veterans, and the middle class.

Although Hitler had terminated his Austrian citizenship in 1925, he did not acquire German citizenship for almost seven years. This meant that he was stateless, legally unable to run for public office, and still faced the risk of deportation. On 25th February 1932, the interior minister of Brunswick, Dietrich Klagges, who was a member of the Nazi Party, appointed Hitler as administrator for the state's delegation to the Reichsrat in Berlin, making Hitler a citizen of Brunswick, and thus of Germany.

Hitler ran against Hindenburg in the 1932 presidential elections. A speech to the **Industry Club in Düsseldorf** on 27th January 1932 won him support from many of Germany's most powerful industrialists. Hindenburg had support from various nationalist, monarchist, Catholic, and republican parties, and some Social Democrats. Hitler used the campaign slogan **"Hitler über Deutschland"** ("Hitler over Germany"), a reference to his political ambitions and his campaigning by aircraft. He was one of the first politicians to use aircraft travel for political purposes, and used it effectively. Hitler came in second in both rounds of the election, garnering more than 35 per cent of the vote in the final election. Although he lost to Hindenburg, this election established Hitler as a strong force in German politics.

Appointment as Chancellor

The absence of an effective government prompted two influential politicians, **Franz von Papen** and **Alfred Hugenberg**, along with several other industrialists and businessmen, to write a letter to Hindenburg. The signers urged Hindenburg to appoint Hitler as leader of a government "independent from parliamentary parties", which could turn into a movement that would "enrapture millions of people".

Hindenburg reluctantly agreed to appoint Hitler as chancellor after two further parliamentary elections—in July and November 1932—had not resulted in the formation of a majority government. Hitler headed a short-lived coalition government formed by the Nazi Party (which had the most seats in the Reichstag) and Hugenberg's party, the German National People's Party (DNVP). On 30th January 1933, the new cabinet was sworn in during a brief ceremony in Hindenburg's office. The Nazi Party gained three posts: Hitler was named chancellor, Wilhelm Frick Minister of the Interior, and Hermann Göring Minister of the Interior for Prussia. Hitler had insisted on the ministerial positions as a way to gain control over the police in much of Germany.

Reichstag Fire and March Elections

As chancellor, Hitler worked against attempts by the Nazi Party's opponents to build a majority government. Because of the political stalemate, he asked Hindenburg to again dissolve the Reichstag, and elections were scheduled for early March. On 27th February 1933, the Reichstag building was set on fire. Göring blamed a communist plot, as Dutch communist **Marinus van der Lubbe** was found in incriminating circumstances inside the burning building. Until the 1960s, some historians including William L. Shirer and Alan Bullock thought the Nazi Party itself was responsible; the current consensus of nearly all historians is that van der Lubbe actually set the fire alone. At Hitler's urging, Hindenburg responded by signing the **Reichstag Fire Decree** of 28th February, drafted by the Nazis, which suspended basic rights and allowed detention without trial. The decree was permitted under Article 48 of the Weimar Constitution, which gave the president the power to take emergency measures to protect public safety and order. Activities of the German Communist Party (KPD) were suppressed, and some 4,000 KPD members were arrested.

In addition to political campaigning, the Nazi Party engaged in paramilitary violence and the spread of anti-communist propaganda in the days preceding the election. On the election day, 6th March 1933, the Nazi Party's share of the vote increased to 43.9 per cent, and the party acquired the largest number of seats in parliament. Hitler's party failed to secure an absolute majority, necessitating another coalition with the DNVP.

Day of Potsdam and the Enabling Act

On 21st March 1933, the new Reichstag was constituted with an opening ceremony at the Garrison Church in Potsdam. This "Day of Potsdam" was held to demonstrate unity between the Nazi movement and the old Prussian elite and military. Hitler appeared in a morning coat and humbly greeted Hindenburg.

To achieve full political control despite not having an absolute majority in parliament, Hitler's government brought the **Ermächtigungsgesetz** (Enabling Act) to a vote in the newly elected Reichstag. The Act – officially titled the **Gesetz zur Behebung der Not von Volk und Reich** ("Law to Remedy the Distress of People and Reich") – gave Hitler's cabinet the power to enact laws without the consent of the Reichstag for four years. These laws could (with certain exceptions) deviate from the constitution. Since it would affect the constitution, the Enabling Act required a two-thirds majority to pass. Leaving nothing to chance, the Nazis used the provisions of the Reichstag Fire Decree to arrest all 81 Communist deputies (in spite of their virulent campaign against the party, the Nazis had allowed the KPD to contest the election) and prevent several Social Democrats from attending.

On 23rd March 1933, the Reichstag assembled at the **Kroll Opera House** under turbulent circumstances. Ranks of SA men served as guards inside the building, while large groups outside opposing the proposed legislation shouted slogans and threats towards the arriving members of parliament. After Hitler verbally promised Centre party leader Ludwig Kaas that Hindenburg would retain his power of veto, Kaas announced the Centre Party would support the Enabling Act. The Act passed by a vote of 444–94, with all parties except the Social Democrats voting in favour. The **Enabling Act**, along with the **Reichstag Fire Decree**, transformed Hitler's government into a de facto legal dictatorship.

Dictatorship

Having achieved full control over the legislative and executive branches of government, Hitler and his allies began to suppress the remaining opposition. The Social Democratic Party was banned and its assets seized. While many trade union delegates were in Berlin for May Day activities, **SA stormtroopers** occupied union offices around the country. On 2nd May 1933, all trade unions were forced to dissolve and their leaders were arrested. Some were sent to concentration camps. The German Labour

Front was formed as an umbrella organisation to represent all workers, administrators, and company owners, thus reflecting the concept of Nazism in the spirit of Hitler's **Volksgemeinschaft** ("people's community").

By the end of June, the other parties had been intimidated into disbanding. This included the Nazis' nominal coalition partner, the DNVP; with the SA's help, Hitler forced its leader, Hugenberg, to resign on 29th June. On 14th July 1933, the Nazi Party was declared the only legal political party in Germany. The demands of the SA for more political and military power caused anxiety among military, industrial, and political leaders. In response, Hitler purged the entire SA leadership in the Night of the Long Knives, which took place from 30th June to 2nd July 1934. Hitler targeted Ernst Röhm and other SA leaders who, along with a number of Hitler's political adversaries (such as Gregor Strasser and former chancellor Kurt von Schleicher), were rounded up, arrested, and shot. While the international community and some Germans were shocked by the murders, many in Germany believed Hitler was restoring order.

On 2nd August 1934, Hindenburg died. The previous day, the cabinet had enacted the Law Concerning the Head of State of the German Reich. This law stated that upon Hindenburg's death, the office of president would be abolished and its powers merged with those of the chancellor. Hitler thus became head of state as well as head of government, and was formally named as **Führer und Reichskanzler** (leader and chancellor), although Reichskanzler was eventually quietly dropped. With this action, Hitler eliminated the last legal remedy by which he could be removed from office.

As head of state, Hitler became commander-in-chief of the armed forces. Immediately after Hindenburg's death, at the instigation of the leadership of the Reichswehr, the traditional loyalty oath of soldiers was altered to affirm loyalty to Hitler personally, by name, rather than to the office of commander-in-chief (which was later renamed to supreme commander) or the state. On 19th August, the merger of the presidency with the chancellorship was approved by 88 per cent of the electorate voting in a plebiscite.

In early 1938, Hitler used blackmail to consolidate his hold over the military by instigating the **Blomberg–Fritsch affair.** Hitler forced his War Minister, Field Marshal Werner von Blomberg, to resign by using a police dossier that showed that Blomberg's new wife had a record for prostitution. Army commander Colonel-General Werner von Fritsch was removed after the Schutzstaffel (SS) produced allegations that he had engaged in a homosexual relationship. Both men had fallen into disfavour because they objected to Hitler's demand to make the Wehrmacht ready for war as early as 1938. Hitler assumed **Blomberg's title of Commander-in-Chief**, thus taking personal command of the armed forces. He replaced the Ministry of War with the Oberkommando der Wehrmacht (OKW), headed by General Wilhelm Keitel. On the same day, sixteen generals were stripped of their commands and 44 more were transferred; all were suspected of not being sufficiently pro-Nazi. By early February 1938, twelve more generals had been removed.

Hitler took care to give his dictatorship the appearance of legality. Many of his decrees were explicitly based on the Reichstag Fire Decree and hence on Article 48 of the Weimar Constitution. The Reichstag renewed the Enabling Act twice, each time for a four-year period. While elections to the Reichstag were still held (in 1933, 1936, and 1938), voters were presented with a single list of Nazis and pro-Nazi "guests" which carried with well over 90 per cent of the vote. These elections were held in far-from-secret conditions; the Nazis threatened severe reprisals against anyone who did not vote or dared to vote.

Nazi Germany

Economy and Culture

In August 1934, Hitler appointed Reichsbank President Hjalmar Schacht as Minister of Economics, and in the following year, as Plenipotentiary for War Economy in charge of preparing the economy for war. Reconstruction and rearmament were financed through Mefo bills, printing money, and seizing the assets of people arrested as enemies of the State, including Jews. Unemployment fell from six million in 1932 to one million in 1936. Hitler oversaw one of the largest infrastructure improvement campaigns in German history, leading to the construction of dams, autobahns, railroads, and other civil works. Wages were slightly lower in the mid to late 1930s compared with wages during the Weimar Republic, while the cost of living increased by 25 per cent. The average work week increased during the shift to a war economy; by 1939, the average German was working between 47 and 50 hours a week.

Hitler's government sponsored architecture on an immense scale. **Albert Speer**, instrumental in implementing Hitler's classicist reinterpretation of German culture, was placed in charge of the proposed architectural renovations of Berlin. Despite a threatened multi-nation boycott, Germany hosted the 1936 Olympic Games. Hitler officiated at the opening ceremonies and attended events at both the **Winter Games** in Garmisch-Partenkirchen and the **Summer Games** in Berlin.

Rearmament and New Alliances

In a meeting with German military leaders on 3rd February 1933, Hitler spoke of "conquest for Lebensraum in the East and its ruthless Germanisation" as his ultimate foreign policy objectives. In March, Prince Bernhard Wilhelm von Bülow, secretary at the Auswärtiges Amt (Foreign Office), issued a statement of major foreign policy aims: Anschluss with Austria, the restoration of Germany's national borders of 1914, rejection of military restrictions under the Treaty of Versailles, the return of the former German colonies in Africa, and a German zone of influence in Eastern Europe. Hitler found **Bülow's goals** to be too modest. In speeches during this period, he stressed the peaceful goals of his policies and a willingness to work within international agreements. At the first meeting of his cabinet in 1933, Hitler prioritised military spending over unemployment relief.

Germany withdrew from the League of Nations and the World Disarmament Conference in October 1933. In January 1935, over 90 per cent of the people of the Saarland, then under League of Nations administration, voted to unite with Germany. That March, Hitler announced an expansion of the **Wehrmacht** to 600,000 members – six times the number permitted by the Versailles Treaty – including development of an air force **(Luftwaffe)** and an increase in the size of the navy **(Kriegsmarine)**. Britain, France, Italy, and the League of Nations condemned these violations of the Treaty, but did nothing to stop it. The **Anglo-German Naval Agreement (AGNA)** of 18th June allowed German tonnage to increase to 35 per cent of that of the British navy. Hitler called the signing of the AGNA "the happiest day of his life", believing that the agreement marked the beginning of the Anglo-German alliance he had predicted in **'Mein Kampf.'** France and Italy were not consulted before the signing, directly undermining the League of Nations and setting the Treaty of Versailles on the path towards irrelevance.

Germany reoccupied the demilitarised zone in the Rhineland in March 1936, in violation of the Versailles Treaty. Hitler also sent troops to Spain to support General Franco during the Spanish Civil War after receiving an appeal for help in July 1936. At the same time, Hitler continued his efforts to create an Anglo-German alliance. In August 1936, in response to a growing economic crisis caused by his rearmament efforts, Hitler ordered Göring to implement a **Four Year Plan** to prepare Germany for war within the next four years. The plan envisaged an all-out struggle between "Judeo-Bolshevism" and German Nazism, which in Hitler's view required a committed effort of rearmament regardless of the economic costs.

In October 1936, Count Galeazzo Ciano, foreign minister of Mussolini's government, visited Germany, where he signed a **Nine-Point Protocol** as an expression of rapprochement and had a personal meeting with Hitler. On 1st November, Mussolini declared an "axis" between Germany and Italy. On 25th November, Germany signed the **Anti-Comintern Pact** with Japan. Britain, China, Italy, and Poland were also invited to join the Anti-Comintern Pact, but only Italy signed in 1937. Hitler abandoned his plan of an Anglo-German alliance, blaming "inadequate" British leadership. At a meeting in the Reich Chancellery with his foreign ministers and military chiefs that November, Hitler restated his intention of acquiring Lebensraum for the German people. He ordered preparations for war in the East, to begin as early as 1938 and no later than 1943. In the event of his death, the conference minutes, recorded as the **Hossbach Memorandum**, were to be regarded as his "political testament". He felt that a severe decline in living standards in Germany as a result of the economic crisis could only be stopped by military aggression aimed at seizing Austria and Czechoslovakia. Hitler urged quick action before Britain and France gained a permanent lead in the arms race. In early 1938, in the wake of the Blomberg–Fritsch affair, Hitler asserted control of the military-foreign policy apparatus, dismissing Neurath as foreign minister and appointing himself as War Minister. From early 1938 onwards, Hitler was carrying out a foreign policy ultimately aimed at war.

Chapter - 5

World War II
Early Diplomatic Successes

Alliance with Japan

In February 1938, on the advice of his newly appointed foreign minister, the strongly pro-Japanese Joachim von Ribbentrop, Hitler ended the **Sino-German alliance** with the Republic of China to enter into an alliance with the more modern and powerful **empire of Japan**. Hitler announced German recognition of **Manchukuo**, the Japanese-occupied state in Manchuria, and renounced German claims to their former colonies in the Pacific held by Japan. Hitler ordered an end to arms shipments to China and recalled all German officers working with the Chinese Army. In retaliation, Chinese General, Chiang Kai-shek cancelled all Sino-German economic agreements, depriving the Germans of many Chinese raw materials.

Austria and Czechoslovakia

On 12th March 1938, Hitler announced the unification of Austria with Nazi Germany in the Anschluss. Hitler then turned his attention to the ethnic German population of the Sudetenland region of Czechoslovakia. On 28–29th March 1938, Hitler held a series of secret meetings in Berlin with **Konrad Henlein** of the Sudeten German Party, the largest of the ethnic German parties of the Sudetenland. The men agreed that Henlein would demand increased autonomy for Sudeten Germans from the Czechoslovakian government, thus providing a pretext for German military action against Czechoslovakia. In April 1938 Henlein told the foreign minister of Hungary that "whatever the Czech government might offer, he would always raise still higher demands ... he wanted to sabotage an understanding by any means because this was the only method to blow up Czechoslovakia quickly". In private, Hitler considered the Sudeten issue unimportant; his real intention was a war of conquest against Czechoslovakia.

In April, Hitler ordered the OKW to prepare for **Fall Grün** (Case Green), the code name for an invasion of Czechoslovakia. As a result of intense French and British diplomatic pressure, on 5th September Czechoslovakian President Edvard Beneš unveiled the "Fourth Plan" for constitutional reorganisation of his country, which agreed to most of Henlein's demands for Sudeten autonomy. Henlein's party responded to Beneš' offer by instigating a series of violent clashes with the Czechoslovakian police that led to the declaration of martial law in certain Sudeten districts.

Germany was dependent on imported oil; a confrontation with Britain over the Czechoslovakian dispute could curtail Germany's oil supplies. This forced Hitler to call off Fall Grün, originally planned for 1st October 1938. On 29th September Hitler, Neville Chamberlain, Édouard Daladier, and Mussolini attended a one-day conference in Munich that led to the Munich Agreement, which handed over the Sudetenland districts to Germany.

Chamberlain was satisfied with the Munich conference, calling the outcome "peace for our time", while Hitler was angered about the missed opportunity for war in 1938; he expressed his disappointment in a speech on 9th October in Saarbrücken. In Hitler's view, the British-brokered peace, although favourable to the ostensible German demands, was a diplomatic defeat which spurred his intent of limiting British power to pave the way for the eastern expansion of Germany. As a result of the summit, Hitler was selected Time magazine's **Man of the Year** for 1938.

In late 1938 and early 1939, the continuing economic crisis caused by rearmament forced Hitler to make major defence cuts. In his **"Export or die"** speech of 30th January 1939, he called for an economic offensive to increase German foreign exchange holdings to pay for raw materials such as high-grade iron needed for military weapons.

On 14th March 1939, under threat from Hungary, Slovakia declared independence and received protection from Germany. The next day, in violation of the Munich accord and possibly as a result of the deepening economic crisis requiring additional assets, Hitler ordered the **Wehrmacht** to invade the Czech rump state, and from Prague Castle he proclaimed the territory a German protectorate.

Beginning of World War II

In private discussions in 1939, Hitler declared Britain the main enemy to be defeated and that Poland's obliteration was a necessary prelude for that goal. The eastern flank would be secured and land would be added to Germany's **Lebensraum**. Offended by the British "guarantee" on 31st March 1939 of Polish independence, he said, "I shall brew them a devil's drink". In a speech in Wilhelmshaven for the launch of the battleship Tirpitz on 1st April, he threatened to denounce the **Anglo-German Naval Agreement** if the British continued to guarantee Polish independence, which he perceived as an "encirclement" policy. Poland was to either become a German satellite state or it would be neutralised in order to secure the Reich's eastern flank and prevent a possible British blockade. Hitler initially favoured the idea of a satellite state, but upon its rejection by the Polish government, he decided to invade and made this the main foreign policy goal of 1939. On 3rd April, Hitler ordered the military to prepare for **Fall Weiss** ("Case White"), the plan for invading Poland on 25th August. In a Reichstag speech on 28th April, he renounced both the **Anglo-German Naval Agreement** and the **German–Polish Non-Aggression Pact.**

Historians such as William Carr, Gerhard Weinberg, and Ian Kershaw have argued that one reason for Hitler's rush to war was his fear of an early death. He had repeatedly claimed that he must lead Germany into war before he got too old, as his successors might lack his strength of will.

Hitler was concerned that a military attack against Poland could result in a premature war with Britain. Hitler's foreign minister and former Ambassador to London, **Joachim von Ribbentrop**, assured him that neither Britain nor France would honour their commitments to Poland. Accordingly, on 22nd August 1939 Hitler ordered a military mobilisation against Poland.

This plan required tacit Soviet support and the non-aggression pact **(the Molotov–Ribbentrop Pact)** between Germany and the Soviet Union, led by Joseph Stalin, included a secret agreement to partition Poland between the two countries. Contrary to Ribbentrop's prediction that Britain would sever Anglo-Polish ties, Britain and Poland signed the **Anglo-Polish alliance** on 25th August 1939. This, along with news from Italy that Mussolini would not honour the **Pact of Steel,** prompted Hitler to postpone the attack on Poland from 25th August to 1st September. Hitler unsuccessfully tried to manoeuvre the British into neutrality by offering them a non-aggression guarantee on 25th August; he then instructed Ribbentrop to present a last-minute peace plan with an impossibly short time limit in an effort to blame the imminent war on British and Polish inaction.

On 1st September 1939, Germany invaded western Poland under the pretext of having been denied claims to the Free City of Danzig and the right to extraterritorial roads across the Polish Corridor, which Germany had ceded under the Versailles Treaty. In response, Britain and France declared war on Germany on 3rd September, surprising Hitler and prompting him to angrily ask Ribbentrop, "Now what?" France and Britain did not act on their declarations immediately, and on 17th September, Soviet forces invaded eastern Poland.

The fall of Poland was followed by what contemporary journalists dubbed the **"Phoney War"** or **Sitzkrieg ("sitting war")**. Hitler instructed the two newly appointed Gauleiters of north-western Poland, **Albert Forster of Reichsgau Danzig-West Prussia** and **Arthur Greiser of Reichsgau Wartheland**, to Germanise their areas, with "no questions asked" about how this was accomplished. In Forster's area, ethnic Poles merely had to sign forms stating that they had German blood. In contrast, Greiser agreed with Himmler and carried out an ethnic cleansing campaign towards Poles. Greiser soon complained that Forster was allowing thousands of Poles to be accepted as "racial" Germans and thus endangered German "racial purity". Hitler refrained from getting involved. This inaction has been advanced as an example of the theory of "working towards the Führer", in which Hitler issued vague instructions and expected his subordinates to work out policies on their own.

Another dispute pitched one side represented by Heinrich Himmler and Greiser, who championed ethnic cleansing in Poland, against another represented by Göring and Hans Frank (governor-general of occupied

Poland), who called for turning Poland into the "granary" of the Reich. On 12th February 1940, the dispute was initially settled in favour of the Göring–Frank view, which ended the economically disruptive mass expulsions. On 15th May 1940, Himmler issued a memo entitled **"Some Thoughts on the Treatment of Alien Population in the East"**, calling for the expulsion of the entire Jewish population of Europe into Africa and the reduction of the Polish population to a "leaderless class of labourers". Hitler called Himmler's memo "good and correct", and, ignoring Göring and Frank, implemented the **Himmler–Greiser** policy in Poland.

On 9th April, German forces invaded Denmark and Norway. On the same day Hitler proclaimed the birth of the **Greater Germanic Reich**, his vision of a united empire of Germanic nations of Europe in which the Dutch, Flemish, and Scandinavians were joined into a "racially pure" polity under German leadership. In May 1940, Germany attacked France, and conquered Luxembourg, the Netherlands, and Belgium. These victories prompted Mussolini to have Italy join forces with Hitler on 10th June. France and Germany signed an armistice on 22nd June. Kershaw notes that Hitler's popularity within Germany – and German support for the war – reached its peak when he returned to Berlin on 6th July from his tour of Paris. Following the unexpected swift victory, Hitler promoted twelve generals to the rank of field marshal during the 1940 Field Marshal Ceremony.

Britain, whose troops were forced to evacuate France by sea from Dunkirk, continued to fight alongside other British dominions in the Battle of the Atlantic. Hitler made peace overtures to the new British leader, Winston Churchill, and upon their rejection he ordered a series of aerial attacks on Royal Air Force airbases and radar stations in southeast England. On 7th September the systematic nightly bombing of London began. The German Luftwaffe failed to defeat the Royal Air Force in what became known as the **Battle of Britain.** By the end of September, Hitler realised that air superiority for the invasion of Britain (in Operation Sea Lion) could not be achieved, and ordered the operation postponed. The nightly air raids on British cities intensified and continued for months, including London, Plymouth, and Coventry.

On 27th September 1940, the **Tripartite Pact** was signed in Berlin by Saburō Kurusu of Imperial Japan, Hitler, and Italian foreign minister Ciano, and later expanded to include Hungary, Romania, and Bulgaria, thus yielding the Axis powers. Hitler's attempt to integrate the Soviet

Union into the anti-British bloc failed after inconclusive talks between Hitler and Molotov in Berlin in November, and he ordered preparations for the invasion of the Soviet Union.

In early 1941, German forces were deployed to North Africa, the Balkans, and the Middle East. In February, German forces arrived in Libya to bolster the Italian presence. In April, Hitler launched the invasion of Yugoslavia, quickly followed by the invasion of Greece. In May, German forces were sent to support Iraqi forces fighting against the British and to invade Crete.

Road to Defeat

On 22nd June 1941, contravening the **Molotov–Ribbentrop Pact** of 1939, over three million Axis troops attacked the Soviet Union. This offensive (code named **Operation Barbarossa**) was intended to destroy the Soviet Union and seize its natural resources for subsequent aggression against the Western powers. The invasion conquered a huge area, including the Baltic republics, Belarus, and West Ukraine. By early August, Axis troops had advanced 500 km and won the **Battle of Smolensk**. Hitler ordered Army Group Centre to temporarily halt its advance to Moscow and divert its Panzer groups to aid in the encirclement of Leningrad and Kiev. His generals disagreed with this change, having advanced within 400 km of Moscow, and his decision caused a crisis among the military leadership. The pause provided the **Red Army** with an opportunity to mobilise fresh reserves. During this crisis, Hitler appointed himself as head of the Oberkommando des Heeres.

On 7th December 1941, Japan attacked the American fleet based at **Pearl Harbor**, Hawaii. Four days later, Hitler declared war against the United States. On 18th December 1941, Himmler asked Hitler, "What to do with the Jews of Russia?", to which Hitler replied, "als Partisanen auszurotten" ("exterminate them as partisans").

In late 1942, German forces were defeated in the second battle of **El Alamein,** thwarting Hitler's plans to seize the Suez Canal and the Middle East. Overconfident in his own military expertise following the earlier victories in 1940, Hitler became distrustful of his Army High Command and began to interfere in military and tactical planning, with damaging consequences. In December 1942 and January 1943, Hitler's repeated refusal to allow their withdrawal at the **Battle of Stalingrad** led to the almost total destruction of the 6th Army. Over 200,000 Axis soldiers were killed and 235,000 were taken prisoner. Thereafter came a decisive strategic defeat at the **Battle of Kursk.** Hitler's military judgement became increasingly erratic, and Germany's military and economic position deteriorated, as did Hitler's health.

Following the Allied invasion of Sicily in 1943, Mussolini was removed from power by King Victor Emmanuel III after a vote of no confidence of the Grand Council of Fascism. Marshal Pietro Badoglio, placed in charge of the government, soon surrendered to the Allies. Throughout 1943 and 1944, the Soviet Union steadily forced Hitler's armies into retreat along the Eastern Front. On 6th June 1944, the Western Allied armies landed in northern France in one of the largest amphibious operations in history, **Operation Overlord.** Many German officers concluded that defeat was inevitable and that continuing under Hitler's leadership would result in the complete destruction of the country.

Between 1939 and 1945, there were many plans to assassinate Hitler, some of which proceeded to significant degrees. The most well known, the 20th July plot of 1944, came from within Germany and was at least partly driven by the increasing prospect of a German defeat in the war. Part of **Operation Valkyrie,** the plot involved Claus von Stauffenberg planting a bomb in one of Hitler's headquarters, the Wolf's Lair at Rastenburg. Hitler narrowly survived because staff officer Heinz Brandt moved the briefcase containing the bomb behind a leg of the heavy conference table, which deflected much of the blast. Later, Hitler ordered savage reprisals resulting in the execution of more than 4,900 people.

According to British academic Dan Plesch, Hitler was put on the United Nations War Crimes Commission's first list of war criminals in December 1944, after determining that Hitler could be held criminally responsible for the acts of the Nazis in occupied countries. By March 1945 at least seven indictments had been filed against him.

Chapter - 6

Hitler's Defeat and Death

By late 1944, both the **Red Army** and the **Western Allies** were advancing into Germany. Recognising the strength and determination of the Red Army, Hitler decided to use his remaining mobile reserves against the American and British armies, which he perceived as far weaker. On 16th December, he launched the **Ardennes Offensive** to incite disunity among the Western Allies and perhaps convince them to join his fight against the Soviets. After some temporary successes, the offensive failed.

With much of Germany in ruins in January 1945, Hitler spoke on the radio: "However grave as the crisis may be at this moment, it will, despite everything, be mastered by our unalterable will." Acting on his view that Germany's military failures meant it had forfeited its right to survive as a nation, Hitler ordered the destruction of all German industrial infrastructure before it could fall into Allied hands. The Minister for Armaments, Albert Speer was entrusted with executing this scorched earth policy, but he secretly disobeyed the order. Hitler's hope to negotiate peace with the United States and Britain was encouraged by the death of US President Franklin D. Roosevelt on 12th April 1945, but contrary to his expectations, this caused no rift among the Allies.

On 20th April, on his 56th birthday, Hitler made his last trip from the **Führerbunker** (Führer's shelter) to the surface. In the ruined garden of the Reich Chancellery, he awarded **Iron Crosses** to boy soldiers of the **Hitler Youth**, who were now fighting the Red Army at the front near Berlin. By 21st April, Georgy Zhukov's 1st Belorussian Front had broken through the defences of General Gotthard Heinrici's Army Group Vistula during the **Battle of the Seelow Heights** and advanced to the outskirts of Berlin. In denial about the dire situation, Hitler placed his hopes on the undermanned and under-equipped Armeeabteilung Steiner (Army Detachment Steiner), commanded by Felix Steiner. Hitler ordered Steiner to attack the northern flank of the salient, while the German Ninth Army was ordered to attack northward in a pincer attack.

During a military conference on 22nd April, Hitler asked about Steiner's offensive. He was told that the attack had not been launched and that the Soviets had entered Berlin. Hitler asked everyone except Wilhelm Keitel, Alfred Jodl, Hans Krebs, and Wilhelm Burgdorf to leave the room, then launched into a tirade against the treachery and incompetence of his commanders, culminating in his declaration—for the first time—that "everything was lost". He announced that he would stay in Berlin until the end and then shoot himself.

By 23rd April the Red Army had surrounded Berlin, and Goebbels made a proclamation urging its citizens to defend the city. That same day, Göring sent a telegram from Berchtesgaden, arguing that since Hitler was isolated in Berlin, Göring should assume leadership of Germany. Göring set a deadline, after which he would consider Hitler incapacitated. Hitler responded by having Göring arrested, and in his last will and testament of 29th April, he removed Göring from all government positions. On 28th April Hitler discovered that Himmler, who had left Berlin on 20th April, was trying to negotiate a surrender to the Western Allies. He ordered Himmler's arrest and had Hermann Fegelein shot.

After midnight on the night of 28–29th April, **Hitler married Eva Braun** in a small civil ceremony in the Führerbunker. Later that afternoon, Hitler was informed that Mussolini had been executed by the Italian resistance movement on the previous day.

On 30th April 1945, Soviet troops were within a block or two of the Reich Chancellery **when Hitler shot himself in the head** and **Braun bit into a cyanide capsule**. Carrying out Hitler's previous command, their corpses were carried outside to the garden behind the Reich Chancellery, where they were placed in a bomb crater, doused with petrol, and set on fire as the Red Army shelling continued. Grand Admiral Karl Dönitz and Joseph Goebbels assumed Hitler's roles as head of state and chancellor respectively.

Berlin surrendered on 2nd May. The remains of Joseph and Magda Goebbels, the six Goebbels children, General Hans Krebs, and Hitler's dogs were repeatedly buried and exhumed. Hitler and Braun's remains were alleged to have been moved as well. There is no evidence that any actual bodily remains of Hitler or Braun—with the exception of dental bridges—were found by the Soviets, which could be identified as their remains. While news of Hitler's death spread quickly, a death certificate was not issued until 1956, after a lengthy investigation to collect testimony from 42 witnesses. Hitler's demise was entered as an assumption of death based on this testimony.

Chapter - 7

The Holocaust

The Holocaust (1933–1945) was the systematic, state-sponsored persecution and murder of six million European Jews by the Nazi German regime and its allies and collaborators. The Holocaust began in January 1933 when Adolf Hitler and the Nazi Party came to power in Germany. It ended in May 1945, when the Allied Powers defeated Nazi Germany in World War II. The Holocaust is also sometimes referred to as **"the Shoah"** the Hebrew word for **"catastrophe."**

When the Nazis came to power in Germany, they did not immediately carry out mass murder. However, they quickly began using the government to target and exclude Jews from German society. Among other anti-semitic measures, the Nazi German regime enacted discriminatory laws and organized violence targeting Germany's Jews. The Nazi persecution of Jews became increasingly radical between 1933 and 1945. This radicalization culminated in a plan that Nazi leaders referred to as the **"Final Solution to the Jewish Question."** The "Final Solution" was the organized and systematic mass murder of

European Jews. The Nazi German regime implemented this genocide between 1941 and 1945.

Why did the Nazis target Jews?

The Nazis targeted Jews because the Nazis were radically anti-semitic. This means that they were prejudiced against and hated Jews. In fact, anti-semitism was a basic tenet of their ideology and the foundation of their worldview.

The Nazis falsely accused Jews of causing Germany's social, economic, political and cultural problems. In particular, they blamed them for Germany's defeat in World War I (1914–1918). Some Germans were receptive to these Nazi claims. Anger over the loss of the war and the economic and political crises that followed contributed to increasing anti-semitism in German society. The instability of Germany under the **Weimar Republic** (1918–1933), the fear of communism, and the economic shocks of the Great Depression also made many Germans more open to Nazi ideas, including anti-semitism.

However, the Nazis did not invent anti-semitism. Anti-semitism is an old and widespread prejudice that has taken many forms throughout history. In Europe, it dates back to ancient times. In the Middle Ages (500–1400), prejudices against Jews were primarily based in early Christian belief and thought, particularly the myth that Jews were responsible for the death of Jesus. Suspicion and discrimination rooted in religious prejudices continued in early modern Europe (1400–1800). At that time, leaders in much of Christian Europe isolated Jews from most aspects of economic, social, and political life. This exclusion contributed to stereotypes of Jews as outsiders. As Europe became more secular, many places lifted most legal restrictions on Jews. This, however, did not mean the end of anti-semitism. In addition to religious anti-semitism, other types of anti-semitism took hold in Europe in the 18th and 19th centuries. These new forms included economic, nationalist, and racial anti-semitism. In the 19th century, anti-semites falsely claimed that Jews were responsible for many social and political ills in modern, industrial society. Theories of race, eugenics, and social Darwinism falsely justified these hatreds. Nazi prejudice against Jews drew upon all of these elements, but especially racial anti-semitism. Racial anti-semitism is the discriminatory idea that Jews are a separate and inferior race.

 THE RISE OF ADOLF HITLER

The Nazi Party promoted a particularly virulent form of racial anti-semitism. It was central to the party's race-based worldview. The Nazis believed that the world was divided into distinct races and that some of these races were superior to others. They considered Germans to be members of the supposedly superior "Aryan" race. They asserted that "Aryans" were locked in a struggle for existence with other, inferior races. Further, the Nazis believed that the so-called "Jewish race" was the most inferior and dangerous of all. According to the Nazis, Jews were a threat that needed to be removed from German society. Otherwise, the Nazis insisted, the "Jewish race" would permanently corrupt and destroy the German people. The Nazis' race-based definition of Jews included many persons who identified as Christians or did not practice Judaism.

Where did the Holocaust take place?

The Holocaust was a Nazi German initiative that took place throughout German- and Axis-controlled Europe. It affected nearly all of Europe's Jewish population, which in 1933 numbered 9 million people.

The Holocaust began in Germany after Adolf Hitler was appointed Chancellor in January 1933. Almost immediately, the Nazi German regime (which called itself the **Third Reich**) excluded Jews from German economic, political, social, and cultural life. Throughout the 1930s, the regime increasingly pressured Jews to emigrate.

But the Nazi persecution of Jews spread beyond Germany. Throughout the 1930s, Nazi Germany pursued an aggressive foreign policy. This culminated in World War II, which began in Europe in 1939. Pre-war and wartime territorial expansion eventually brought millions more Jewish people under German control.

Nazi Germany's territorial expansion began in 1938–1939. During this time, Germany annexed neighboring Austria and the Sudetenland and occupied the Czech lands. On September 1st, 1939, Nazi Germany began World War II (1939–1945) by attacking Poland. Over the next two years, Germany invaded and occupied much of Europe, including western parts of the Soviet Union. Nazi Germany further extended its control by forming alliances with the governments of Italy, Hungary, Romania, and Bulgaria. It also created puppet states in Slovakia and Croatia. Together these countries made up the European members of the Axis alliance, which also included Japan.

By 1942—as a result of annexations, invasions, occupations, and alliances—Nazi Germany controlled most of Europe and parts of North Africa. Nazi control brought harsh policies and ultimately mass murder to Jewish civilians across Europe. The Nazis and their allies and collaborators murdered six million Jews.

How did Nazi Germany and its allies and collaborators persecute Jewish people?

Between 1933 and 1945, Nazi Germany and its allies and collaborators implemented a wide range of anti-Jewish policies and measures. These policies varied from place to place. Thus, not all Jews experienced the Holocaust in the same way. But in all instances, millions of people were persecuted simply because they were identified as Jewish.

Throughout German-controlled and aligned territories, the persecution of Jews took a variety of forms:

- **Legal discrimination in the form of anti-semitic laws**. These included the Nuremberg Race Laws and numerous other discriminatory laws.

- **Various forms of public identification and exclusion**. These included anti-semitic propaganda, boycotts of Jewish-owned businesses, public humiliation, and obligatory markings (such as the Jewish star badge worn as an armband or on clothing).

- **Organized violence**. The most notable example is Kristallnacht. There were also isolated incidents and other pogroms (violent riots).

- **Physical Displacement**. Perpetrators used forced emigration, resettlement, expulsion, deportation, and ghettoization to physically displace Jewish individuals and communities.

- **Internment**. Perpetrators interned Jews in overcrowded ghettos, concentration camps, and forced-labor camps, where many died from starvation, disease, and other inhumane conditions.

- **Widespread theft and plunder**. The confiscation of Jews' property, personal belongings, and valuables was a key part of the Holocaust.

- **Forced labor**. Jews had to perform forced labor in service of the Axis war effort or for the enrichment of Nazi organizations, the military, and/or private businesses.

Many Jews died as a result of these policies. But before 1941, the systematic mass murder of all Jews was not Nazi policy. Beginning in 1941, however, Nazi leaders decided to implement the mass murder of Europe's Jews. They referred to this plan as the "Final Solution to the Jewish Question."

What was the "Final Solution to the Jewish Question"?

The Nazi **"Final Solution to the Jewish Question"** ("Endlösung der Judenfrage") was the deliberate and systematic mass murder of European Jews. It was the last stage of the Holocaust and took place from 1941 to 1945. Though many Jews were killed before the "Final Solution" began, the vast majority of Jewish victims were murdered during this period.

As part of the "Final Solution," Nazi Germany committed mass murder on an unprecedented scale. There were two main methods of killing. One method was mass shooting. German units carried out **mass shootings** on the outskirts of villages, towns, and cities throughout eastern Europe. The other method was **asphyxiation with poison gas**. Gassing operations were conducted at killing centers and with mobile gas vans.

Mass Shootings

The Nazi German regime perpetrated mass shootings of civilians on a scale never seen before. After Germany invaded the Soviet Union in June 1941, German units began to carry out mass shootings of local Jews. At first, these units targeted Jewish men of military age. But by August 1941, they had started massacring entire Jewish communities. These massacres were often conducted in broad daylight and in full view and earshot of local residents.

Mass shooting operations took place in more than 1,500 cities, towns, and villages across eastern Europe. German units tasked with murdering the local Jewish population moved throughout the region committing horrific massacres. Typically, these units would enter a town and round up the Jewish civilians. They would then take the Jewish residents to the outskirts of the town. Next, they would force them to dig a mass grave or take them to mass graves prepared in advance. Finally, German forces and/ or local auxiliary units would shoot all of the men, women, and children into these pits. Sometimes, these massacres involved the use of specially designed mobile gas vans. Perpetrators would use these vans to suffocate victims with carbon monoxide exhaust.

Germans also carried out mass shootings at killing sites in occupied eastern Europe. Typically these were located near large cities. These sites included Fort IX in Kovno (Kaunas), the Rumbula and Bikernieki Forests in Riga, and Maly Trostenets near Minsk. At these killing sites, Germans and local collaborators murdered tens of thousands of Jews from the Kovno, Riga, and Minsk ghettos. They also shot tens of thousands of German, Austrian, and Czech Jews at these killing sites. At Maly Trostenets, thousands of victims were also murdered in gas vans.

The German units that perpetrated the mass shootings in eastern Europe included **Einsatzgruppen** (special task forces of the SS and police), **Order Police battalions,** and **Waffen-SS units**. The German military **(Wehrmacht)** provided logistical support and manpower. Some Wehrmacht units also carried out massacres. In many places, local auxiliary units working with the SS and police participated in the mass shootings. These auxiliary units were made up of local civilian, military, and police officials.

As many as 2 million Jews were murdered in mass shootings or gas vans in territories seized from Soviet forces.

Killing Centers

In late 1941, the Nazi regime began building specially designed, stationary killing centers in German-occupied Poland. These killing centers were sometimes called **"extermination camps"** or **"death camps."** Nazi Germany operated five killing centers: Chelmno, Belzec, Sobibor, Treblinka, and Auschwitz-Birkenau. They built these killing centers for the sole purpose of efficiently murdering Jews on a mass scale. The primary means of murder at the killing centers was poisonous gas released into sealed gas chambers or vans.

German authorities, with the help of their allies and collaborators, transported Jews from across Europe to these killing centers. They disguised their intentions by calling the transports to the killing centers **"resettlement actions"** or **"evacuation transports."** They were often referred to as "deportations." Most of these deportations took place by train. In order to efficiently transport Jews to the killing centers, German authorities used the extensive European railroad system, as well as other means of transportation. In many cases the railcars on the trains were freight cars; in other instances they were passenger cars.

The conditions on deportation transports were horrific. German and collaborating local authorities forced Jews of all ages into overcrowded railcars. They often had to stand, sometimes for days, until the train reached its destination. The perpetrators deprived them of food, water, bathrooms, heat, and medical care. Jews frequently died en route from the inhumane conditions.

The vast majority of Jews deported to killing centers were gassed almost immediately after their arrival. Some Jews whom German officials believed to be healthy and strong enough were selected for forced labor.

At all five killing centers, German officials forced some Jewish prisoners to assist in the killing process. Among other tasks, these prisoners had to sort through victims' belongings and remove victims' bodies from the gas chambers. Special units disposed of the millions of corpses through mass burial, in burning pits, or by burning them in large, specially designed crematoria.

Nearly 2.7 million Jewish men, women, and children were murdered at the five killing centers.

What were ghettos and why did German authorities create them during the Holocaust?

Ghettos were areas of cities or towns where German occupiers forced Jews to live in overcrowded and unsanitary conditions. German authorities often enclosed these areas by building walls or other barriers. Guards prevented Jews from leaving without permission. Some ghettos existed for years, but others existed only for months, weeks, or even days as holding sites prior to deportation or murder.

German officials first created ghettos in 1939–1940 in German-occupied Poland. The two largest were located in the occupied Polish cities of **Warsaw** and **Lodz** (Łódź). Beginning in June 1941, German officials also established them in newly conquered territories in eastern Europe following the German attack on the Soviet Union. German authorities and their allies and collaborators also established ghettos in other parts of Europe. Notably, in 1944, German and Hungarian authorities created temporary ghettos to centralize and control Jews prior to their deportation from Hungary.

The Purpose of the Ghettos

German authorities originally established the ghettos to isolate and control the large local Jewish populations in occupied eastern Europe. Initially, they concentrated Jewish residents from within a city and the surrounding area or region. However, beginning in 1941, German officials also deported Jews from other parts of Europe (including Germany) to some of these ghettos.

Jewish forced labor became a central feature of life in many ghettos. In theory, it was supposed to help pay for the administration of the ghetto as well as support the German war effort. Sometimes, factories and workshops were established nearby in order to exploit the imprisoned Jews for forced labor. The labor was often manual and grueling.

Life in the Ghettos

Life in the ghettos was miserable and dangerous. There was little food and limited sanitation or medical care. Hundreds of thousands of people died by starvation; rampant disease; exposure to extreme temperatures; as well as exhaustion from forced labor. Germans also murdered the imprisoned Jews through brutal beatings, torture, arbitrary shootings, and other forms of arbitrary violence.

The Jews in the ghettos sought to maintain a sense of dignity and community. Schools, libraries, communal welfare services, and religious institutions provided some measure of connection among residents. Many ghettos also had underground movements that carried out armed resistance. The most famous of these is the **Warsaw ghetto** uprising in 1943.

Charlene Schiff describes conditions in the Horochow ghetto.

Both of Charlene's parents were local Jewish community leaders, and the family was active in community life. Charlene's father was a professor of philosophy at the State University of Lvov. World War II began with the German invasion of Poland on September 1st 1939. Charlene's town was in the part of eastern Poland occupied by the Soviet Union under the German-Soviet Pact of August 1939. Under the Soviet occupation, the family remained in its home and Charlene's father continued to teach. The Germans invaded the Soviet Union in June 1941, and arrested

Charlene's father after they occupied the town. She never saw him again. Charlene, her mother, and sister were forced into a ghetto the Germans established in Horochow. In 1942, Charlene and her mother fled from the ghetto after hearing rumors that the Germans were about to destroy it. Her sister attempted to hide separately, but was never heard from again. Charlene and her mother hid in underbrush at the river's edge, and avoided discovery by submerging themselves in the water for part of the time. They hid for several days. One day, Charlene awoke to find that her mother had disappeared. Charlene survived by herself in the forests near Horochow, and was liberated by Soviet troops. She eventually immigrated to the United States.

Liquidating the Ghettos

Beginning in 1941–1942, Germans and their allies and collaborators murdered ghetto residents en masse and dissolved ghetto administrative structures. They called this process **"liquidation."** It was part of the "Final Solution to the Jewish Question." The majority of Jews in the ghettos were murdered either in mass shootings at nearby killing sites or after deportation to killing centers. Most of the killing centers were deliberately located near the large ghettos of German-occupied Poland or on easily-accessible railway routes.

Who was responsible for carrying out the Holocaust and the Final Solution?

Many people were responsible for carrying out the Holocaust and the Final Solution. At the highest level, Adolf Hitler inspired, ordered, approved, and supported the genocide of Europe's Jews. However, Hitler did not act alone. Nor did he lay out an exact plan for the implementation of the Final Solution. Other Nazi leaders were the ones who directly coordinated, planned, and implemented the mass murder. Among them were Hermann Göring, **Heinrich Himmler, Reinhard Heydrich** and **Adolf Eichmann.**

However, millions of Germans and other Europeans participated in the Holocaust. Without their involvement, the genocide of the Jewish people in Europe would not have been possible. Nazi leaders relied upon German institutions and organizations; other Axis powers; local bureaucracies and institutions; and individuals.

German Institutions, Organizations, and Individuals

Nazi leaders relied on many German institutions and organizations to help them carry out the Holocaust. Members of Nazi organizations initiated and carried out many anti-Jewish actions before and during World War II. These organizations included the **Nazi Party, the SA (Stormtroopers or Brownshirts),** and the **SS (Schutzstaffel, Protection Squadron)**. Once the war began, the SS and its police affiliates became especially deadly. Members of the Sicherheitsdienst (the SD), the Gestapo, the Criminal Police (Kripo), and the Order Police played particularly active and deadly roles in the mass murder of Europe's Jews. Other German institutions involved in carrying out the Final Solution included the German military; the German national railway and healthcare systems; the German civil service and criminal justice systems; and German businesses, insurance companies, and banks.

As members of these institutions, countless German soldiers, policemen, civil servants, lawyers, judges, businessmen, engineers, and doctors and nurses chose to implement the regime's policies. Ordinary Germans also participated in the Holocaust in a variety of ways. Some Germans cheered as Jews were beaten or humiliated. Others denounced Jews for disobeying racist laws and regulations. Many Germans bought, took, or looted their Jewish neighbors' belongings and property. These Germans' participation in the Holocaust was motivated by enthusiasm, careerism, fear, greed, self-interest, antisemitism, and political ideals, among other factors.

Non-German Governments and Institutions

Nazi Germany did not perpetrate the Holocaust alone. It relied on the help of its allies and collaborators. In this context, "allies" refers to Axis countries officially allied with Nazi Germany. "Collaborators" refers to regimes and organizations that cooperated with German authorities in an official or semi-official capacity. Nazi Germany's allies and collaborators included:

- **The European Axis Powers and other collaborationist regimes (such as Vichy France).** These governments passed their own anti-semitic legislation and cooperated with German goals.

- **German-backed local bureaucracies, especially local police forces.** These organizations helped round up, intern, and deport Jews even in countries not allied with Germany, such as the Netherlands.

 THE RISE OF ADOLF HITLER

- **Local auxiliary units made up of military and police officials and civilians**. These German-backed units participated in massacres of Jews in eastern Europe (often voluntarily).

The terms "allies" and "collaborators" can also refer to individuals affiliated with these governments and organizations.

Individuals across Europe

Throughout Europe, individuals who had no governmental or institutional affiliation and did not directly participate in murdering Jews also contributed to the Holocaust.

One of the deadliest things that neighbors, acquaintances, colleagues, and even friends could do was denounce Jews to Nazi German authorities. An unknown number chose to do so. They revealed Jews' hiding places, unmasked false Christian identities, and otherwise identified Jews to Nazi officials. In doing so, they brought about their deaths. These individuals' motivations were wide-ranging: fear, self-interest, greed, revenge, antisemitism, and political and ideological beliefs.

Individuals also profited from the Holocaust. Non-Jews sometimes moved into Jews' homes, took over Jewish-owned businesses, and stole Jews' possessions and valuables. This was part of the widespread theft and plunder that accompanied the genocide.

Most often individuals contributed to the Holocaust through inaction and indifference to the plight of their Jewish neighbors. Sometimes these individuals were called bystanders.

Who were the other victims of Nazi persecution and mass murder?

The Holocaust specifically refers to the systematic, state-sponsored persecution and murder of six million Jews. However, there were also millions of other victims of Nazi persecution and murder. In the 1930s, the regime targeted a variety of alleged domestic enemies within German society. As the Nazis extended their reach during World War II, millions of other Europeans were also subjected to Nazi brutality.

The Nazis classified Jews as the priority "enemy." However, they also targeted other groups as threats to the health, unity, and security of the German people. The first group targeted by the Nazi regime consisted of political opponents. These included officials and members of other political parties and trade union activists. Political opponents also included people simply suspected of opposing or criticizing the Nazi regime. Political enemies were the first to be incarcerated in Nazi concentration camps. Jehovah's witnesses were also incarcerated in prisons and concentration camps. They were arrested because they refused to swear loyalty to the government or serve in the German military.

The Nazi regime also targeted Germans whose activities were deemed harmful to German society. These included men accused of homosexuality, persons accused of being professional or habitual criminals, and so-called asocials (such as people identified as vagabonds, beggars, prostitutes, pimps, and alcoholics). Tens of thousands of these victims were incarcerated in prisons and concentration camps. The regime also forcibly sterilized and persecuted Afro-Germans.

People with disabilities were also victimized by the Nazi regime. Before World War II, Germans considered to have supposedly unhealthy hereditary conditions were forcibly sterilized. Once the war began, Nazi policy radicalized. People with disabilities, especially those living in institutions, were considered both a genetic and a financial burden on Germany. These people were targeted for murder in the so-called **Euthanasia Program.**

The Nazi regime employed extreme measures against groups considered to be racial, civilizational, or ideological enemies. This included Roma (Gypsies), Poles (especially the Polish intelligentsia and elites), Soviet officials, and Soviet prisoners of war. The Nazis perpetrated mass murder against these groups.

End of the Holocaust

The Holocaust ended in May 1945 when the major Allied Powers (Great Britain, the United States and the Soviet Union) defeated Nazi Germany in World War II. As Allied forces moved across Europe in a series of offensives, they overran concentration camps. There they liberated the surviving prisoners, many of whom were Jews. The Allies also encountered and liberated the survivors of so-called death marches. These forced marches consisted of groups of Jewish and non-Jewish concentration camp inmates who had been evacuated on foot from camps under SS guard.

But liberation did not bring closure. Many Holocaust survivors faced ongoing threats of violent anti-semitism and displacement as they sought to build new lives. Many had lost family members, while others searched for years to locate missing parents, children and siblings.

How did some Jews survive the Holocaust?

Despite Nazi Germany's efforts to murder all the Jews of Europe, some Jews survived the Holocaust. Survival took a variety of forms. But, in every case, survival was only possible because of an extraordinary confluence of circumstances, choices, help from others (both Jewish and non-Jewish), and sheer luck.

Survival outside of German-Controlled Europe

Some Jews survived the Holocaust by escaping German-controlled Europe. Before World War II began, hundreds of thousands of Jews emigrated from Nazi Germany despite significant immigration barriers. Those who immigrated to the United States, Great Britain, and other areas that remained beyond German control were safe from Nazi violence. Even after World War II began, some Jews managed to escape German-controlled Europe. For example, approximately 200,000 Polish Jews fled the German occupation of Poland. These Jews survived the war under harsh conditions after Soviet authorities deported them further east into the interior of the Soviet Union.

Survival in German-Controlled Europe

A smaller number of Jews survived inside German-controlled Europe. They often did so with the help of rescuers. Rescue efforts ranged from the isolated actions of individuals to organized networks, both small and large. Throughout Europe, there were non-Jews who took grave risks to help their Jewish neighbors, friends, and strangers survive. For example, they found hiding places for Jews, procured false papers that offered protective Christian identities, or provided them with food and supplies. Other Jews survived as members of partisan resistance movements. Finally, some Jews managed, against enormous odds, to survive imprisonment in concentration camps, ghettos, and even killing centers.

Aftermath

While the Holocaust ended with the war, the legacy of terror and genocide did not. By the end of World War II, six million Jews and millions of others were dead. Nazi Germany and its allies and collaborators had devastated or completely destroyed thousands of Jewish communities across Europe.

In the aftermath of the Holocaust, those Jews who survived were often confronted with the traumatic reality of having lost their entire families and communities. Some were able to go home and chose to rebuild their lives in Europe. Many others were afraid to do so because of postwar violence and anti-semitism. In the immediate post-war period, those who could not or would not return home often found themselves living in displaced persons camps. There, many had to wait years before they were able to immigrate to new homes.

Chapter - 8

Leadership Traits of Adolf Hitler

Adolf Hitler did much evil during his regime in Nazi Germany. But he did certain things right as a leader to rally a whole nation.

1. Captivating Public Speaker

Hitler was a captivating public speaker. He would enrapture crowds with his vision and sense of purpose . His words moved a country, even the church to believe that they were killing in the name of God. That was the extent of his charisma. Hitler was a great orator. He gave his nation a new purpose and destiny.

2. Understanding Human Nature

Adolf Hitler understood human nature very well. He knew how to use human nature to his personal gain and with that knowledge, he rallied the whole nation behind him.

3. Constant Influence

Adolf Hitler successfully used propaganda to bring the whole nation under his influence . Through the constant use of media and communications, he managed to cause a whole nation to think alike to serve his cause.

4. Charisma-Passion-Vision

Hitler's charisma was the key to the whole success of National-Socialism, which he was supporting and wanted to pass through the people of Germany. Hitler obtained this charismatic "altitude" partially because of his political skills and appeal.

The enabling factor, which was helping Hitler accomplish almost every task he had, was his surprising clarity of vision. He had great ideas for Germany, to be bigger, better and "purer" than ever but also he was driven by his ego to take over the world, which was not as "pure" as he wanted Germany to be.

Hitler revealed his passion through his speeches. He knew that by arriving late at the meeting point would develop tension among the audience and make them expecting him. When he arrived at the stage he waited for every one to stop talking so as to have total silence. His moves and gestures were so forceful. He walked from side to side at the stage and he gestured with his hands and the tone of his voice was loud and passionate. He was sweating; his face was getting white, his eyes were bulged and his voice was full of emotion. He shouted about the unfairness's and prejudices done to Germany and he made his audience full of hate and jealousy. So by the end his speech ended the crowd was in a condition near to madness and was willing to do everything Hitler was implying.

5. Determination

Hitler's determination and tremendous tenacity of purpose were two characteristics, which described him through his governance. He was a man who was striving for power and command. In order to have the power to be the commander of Germany and conquer the whole world, he managed to climb all the way up from being a simple soldier in the front line to become the chancellor of Germany and the commander of a enormous army. This fact indicates his great will and capability to meet his objectives and to achieve whatever he sought.

6. Integrity

Despite the fact that Hitler was a great leader he had no sense of logical thinking. Hitler's lack of ethical reasoning and social intelligence goes back to his low self-awareness, empathy and interest in others. He was unethical in thoughts and actions, taking advantage of situations, which his followers were in, in the most vicious approach to reach his goals. By manipulating his army to put Jews into extermination camps, is the biggest example not only of his immoral and wicked character but also his twisted mind.

7. Confidence

Hitler was greatly self-assured of his own abilities. His rise in the hierarchy scale, his influential speeches, the fact that he managed to get Germany back from the edge of economic disaster, the battles which he was making in crucial places or in critical time periods are facts which show the huge levels of confidence that Hitler had.

8. Sociability

In terms of Hitler's management towards his secretaries and the people who worked with him closely, Hitler was, surprisingly enough, the more thoughtful boss. In fact, he was adored by those who worked closest with him. His secretaries never became maddened by any kind of rudeness or lack of indulgence towards them. Hitler knew their names and birthdays, he visited them when they were ill, and they repaid him with lifetime loyalty, even after his crimes became generally known.

9. Intelligence

Hitler's intelligence is indisputable. He managed to get Germany back from the edge of economic disaster and made them flourishing again, from a beaten country to a world power in just a few years. The fact that Hitler came from a frontline soldier to the Fuehrer shows not only his great will and capability to meet his objectives but also his great mind sharpness since he was able to manipulate a whole nation in order to do that.

10. Task-oriented

Hitler was a high task-oriented leader. He had clear vision and knowledge of the path to execute his strategy. He wanted to monitor everything and retain control of every task, which was about to be executed. He never blamed himself for his failure which in his case was Germany as a whole.

Hitler's Strategy

Adolf Hitler was a very good strategist. The main point of Hitler's strategy was the accumulation of **Lebensraum ("Living space")** for the Germanic race . Citing the **Treaty of Versailles** suffocating indemnities and exploiting the public nervousness of the 1930s economic lack of money, he declared that the German borders were too restricted to secure their suitable position in the geo-political world relations, and that he wanted regions similar to the (British and French) colonies to secure enough economic resources to assure Germany's position as a major power.

Chapter - 9

Glimpse of Adolf Hitler's Family

The Hitler family comprises relatives and ancestors of Adolf Hitler (20th April 1889 – 30th April 1945. The family has long been of interest to historians and genealogists because of the biological uncertainty of Hitler's paternal grandfather, as well as the family's inter-relationships and their psychological effect on Hitler during his childhood and later life.

The last name "Hitler" has many variations that were often used almost interchangeably. Some of the common variances were Hitler, Hiedler, Hüttler, Hytler, and Hittler. Adolf's father, Alois Schicklgruber changed his name on January 7th 1877, to "Hitler"—the only form of the last name that his son used.

His immediate family tree is filled with multiple marriages. Several children were born illegitimately or only a couple of months after marriage. This gave rise to many disputes such as the contested issue of whether or not Johann Georg Hiedler was Alois Schicklgruber's father.

Adolf Hitler's Parents

Adolf Hitler's father, Alois Schicklgruber had two wives before Adolf's mother. The first, **Anna Glassl-Hörer** (1823–1883) he married in October 1873. Anna became an invalid soon after marriage. In 1880, she filed for a separation and died three years later. Alois and Anna had no children.

Alois' second wife, **Franziska "Fanni" Matzelsberger** (Hitler) married Alois at 19 years of age and gave birth to two children, Alois Jr., and Angela Hitler. Fanni died of tuberculosis at the age of 24.

Not long after Fanni's death, Alois married **Klara Pölzl,** his housekeeper and Adolf's mother, whom he had hired during his first marriage. Klara and Alois had six children together, half of which died before the age of 2. Only Adolf and his youngest sister Paula survived into adulthood. Klara died of breast cancer in 1908 when Adolf was 19-years-old.

Adolf Hitler's Siblings

Although Hitler's immediate family tree lists five full-blood siblings, all of his older siblings died in infancy. Gustav Hitler, born May 17th 1885, died nearly seven months later of diphtheria. The next born, Ida on September 25th 1886, died less than two years later of the same disease. Otto Hitler was born and died in the autumn of 1887. Another of Adolf's siblings, Edmund, was born after Adolf in March 1894 but died of measles at the age of six.

Adolf's youngest sister and only sibling to survive into adulthood was born in 1896 and died of a stroke in 1960. Adolf committed suicide in 1945 and Paula, born in 1896, lived until she died of natural causes in 1960.

From his father's previous marriage, Adolf had two half-siblings, Alois Jr. and Angela Hitler. Both married and had children, some of whom are still alive today. Angela married Leo Raubal and had three children, Adolf's nephew Leo Rudolf (died in 1977) and nieces Angela "Geli" (died in 1931), and Elfriede (died in 1993).

End of the Hitler Bloodline

Two great-nephews from his half-sister Angela's children are still alive as of 2018. After marrying Dr. Ernst Hochegger, Adolf's half-niece Elfriede Hitler Hochegger gave birth to Heiner in 1945. Peter Raubal, the son of Leo Raubal, is currently a retired engineer living in Austria.

According to some reports, the remaining family members have pledged to never have children and end the Hitler bloodline.

Chapter – 10

Alois Hitler: The Story of the Austrian Civil Servant who was Adolf Hitler's Father - Gina Dimuro | Edited By John Kuroski

The father of Adolf Hitler, Alois Hitler was a domineering, unforgiving husband who often beat his wife and his children — leading his son to despise him.

One summer day in a small Austrian village, an unmarried 42-year-old peasant woman gave birth to a baby boy. Considering that this was 1837, it was certainly a minor scandal that the child was born out of wedlock, but Maria Anna Schicklgruber was certainly not the first woman to have found herself in this predicament. In fact, her story would have likely been forgotten entirely had not the son she bore would have the most infamous name in history: Adolf Hitler.

Schicklgruber named her son Alois: his paternity was never established (although there were rumors his father was a wealthy Jewish man his mother had worked for) and he was registered as "illegitimate."

When Alois was about five-years-old, his mother married a millworker who gave Alois his name: Hiedler.

From Alois Hiedler to Alois Hitler

After the death of Alois' mother in 1847, the man believed to be his father, Johann Georg Hiedler, took off. Alois was then left in the care of Hiedler's brother, Johann Nepomuk Hiedler (who some historians speculate might have been his real father). Alois eventually went to Vienna and, to his Johann Nepomuk's immense pride, became an official customs agent. Since Johann Nepomunk had no children of his own, he managed to convince local officials that Johann Georg had named Alois his heir, leaving him to carry on the family name, which the officials misspelled as "Hitler."

The newly-minted Alois Hitler had become locally renown for his fondness for women: he already had an illegitimate daughter of his own by the time he married a wealthy woman 14 years his senior. His first wife was a sickly woman and he thoughtfully hired two young, attractive maids to help around the house: Franziska Matzelsberger and his own 16-year-old cousin, Klara Polzl.

Hitler became involved with both of the girls living under his roof, a situation that led his long-suffering wife to finally file for separation in 1880. Matzelsberger then became the second Mrs. Hitler: much less complacent than her predecessor, one of her first acts as mistress of the household was to send Polzl away. When Franziska died of tuberculosis only a few years later, Polzl made a convenient reappearance.

Alois Hitler wanted to marry his cousin immediately, however, their close relation posed some legal difficulties and they had to request a dispensation from the local bishop. The Bishop was clearly also disturbed by the very few degrees of separation between the pair and forwarded the request to the Vatican, who eventually granted it (perhaps because by this time Klara was already pregnant).

The couple had three children who died in infancy before a son came along who survived. The boy was born on April 20th 1889, and registered as "Adolfus Hitler."

The Father of the Fuhrer

Alois Hitler was a strict father who "demanded absolute obedience" and freely hit his children. A co-worker once described him as "very strict,

    The Rise Of Adolf Hitler

exacting, and pedantic, a most unapproachable person" who obsessed over his official uniform and "always had himself photographed in it." Adolf's half-brother, Alois Jr., described their father as someone who "had no friends, took to no one, and could be very heartless."

In contrast to Klara, who absolutely doted on her son, Alois was quick to give Adolf a "sound thrashing" for the slightest transgression. Hitler later recalled how after a certain point he "resolved never again to cry when my father whipped me" which he claimed caused the beatings to finally end.

Alois Hitler died suddenly of a pleural hemorrhage in 1903 when Adolf was 14-years-old.

The death of his father left Hitler free to pursue his dream of becoming an artist and have his every whim indulged by his mother. Although Hitler later declared "I never loved my father, but feared him," there were striking similarities between father and son besides the uncontrollable fits of rage: the future Fuhrer also strangely employed his own half-niece as a maid and struck up an intimate relationship with her.

Chapter - 11

Letters by Hitler's father found in attic, giving rare glimpses of his early life

The letters were written by Alois Hitler to a road maintenance official called Josef Radlegger, concerning the latter's sale of a farmhouse in the village of Hafeld to Alois in 1895, when Adolf was six-years-old.

"They aren't just letters about business, there's a very familiar atmosphere between the two correspondents and there's a lot of family gossip," Austrian historian, Roman Sandgruber told AFP in the University of Linz's history library, while carefully removing the letters from the bundle they were kept in for decades.

Though Alois was known to be a "very tyrannical head of the family," Sandgruber said the letters also offer an occasional glimpse at congeniality in his home life.

To Alois, his wife Klara was more than the "silent housewife" later described by Adolf in **'Mein Kampf.'**

One of the few people Alois had anything positive to say about, Sandgruber believed her to have been "a thoroughly emancipated woman, as we would put it today."

"One can assume that she certainly had a say in the household," Sandgruber noted, and particularly when it came to money matters.

"My wife... has the necessary enthusiasm and understanding for finances," Alois wrote in one of the letters.

Moreover, the letters are testament to Alois's rise through Austrian society and his dream of becoming a country gentleman with his own farm.

'Genius' complex

The new treasure trove of documents may never have seen the light of day had pensioner Anneliese Smigielski not decided to clear-out and insulate her attic a few years ago.

She had always known that her great-great-grandfather Radlegger had sold property to Alois Hitler, and wasn't particularly surprised to find the letters among more than 500 others, all meticulously kept in boxes.

But after a few attempts to follow Alois's irritable messages — "he seemed to get annoyed about everything" — Smigielski found the sloping Kurrent script too hard to decode and thought it needed the attention of an expert.

Smigielski knew of Sandgruber's previous work on the history of Upper Austria and got in touch with him in 2017, thinking he would be able to make some use of them.

While Alois is known to have made anti-Semitic statements when he himself dabbled in politics later in life, Sandgruber is wary of making too many direct connections between the father's politics and those of his son.

He says the important influence on Adolf was the racist and anti-Semitic currents of thought which were present more generally in the Austria of his childhood.

However, Sandgruber said the one trait which undoubtedly united the two of them was "the very strong influence of being self-taught."

"The result of that is as with the father, the son despised all those who had been through a regular school career — academics, notaries, judges, and later even military officers," he said.

"He thinks that he alone is the genius," Sandgruber added.

He has been taken aback by the international attention his book from an Austrian publisher has received, garnering press coverage as far afield as Peru and China.

Historian Roman Sandgruber holds a letter written by Alois Hitler to road maintenace official Josef Radlegger, in the library of the Johannes Kepler University in Linz, Austria, on March 03, 2021. (ALEX HALADA / AFP)

Smigielski herself also confessed to being a little overwhelmed by the press attention which has followed her attic discovery, saying it feels like "being a hare in the middle of the hunt."

"But it will die down," she said hopefully.

Perhaps not anytime soon though, such is the interest in the book that it entered its second print run just one week after publication on February 22.

Chapter - 12

Religious views of Adolf Hitler

The substance of Adolf Hitler's religious views—along with the relationship of Nazism and religion in general—has been controversial since Hitler appeared on Germany's troubled political scene in the 1920s. Scholars have advanced conflicting opinions, arguing that Hitler was an atheist, a Christian of sorts, an occultist, or a neo-paganist. Historian Richard Weikart has exhaustively examined Hitler's many statements, the testimony of his associates, and the extensive historiographical literature to offer a convincing case that Hitler's religion was in the main pantheism, or something akin to it.

Weikart reaches his conclusion in a series of chapter-length essays that enable him to dismiss various plausible religious options for Hitler's religion. Weikart rightly maintains that Hitler "was a religious chameleon [and] a quintessential religious hypocrite" . Hitler was definitely not a systematic thinker, and he made many seemingly contradictory statements regarding religion. One of the merits of this book is the manner in which Weikart places these statements in their proper context.

Given his freethinking proclivity, his many statements critical of traditional Christianity, and his exaltation of science—with its reputed better claim to knowledge—over religion, it might seem that Hitler was, at his core, an atheist. Weikart demonstrates, however, that in his typically confused manner, Hitler believed "that some kind of God existed." And that "God"—often referred to as "Providence"—would lead Germany to victory, provided the German people would pursue the struggle—a key concept for Hitler—with "determination, will-power, diligence, and the willingness to sacrifice for their racial comrades."

Although confirmed as a Catholic, Hitler was by no means a conventional Christian. He rejected such things as the deity, resurrection, and miracles of Jesus; the Christian ethic of love; the possibility of a personal relationship with God; and any appeal to revelation. Admittedly, he tried to "palm himself off as a Christian when it suited his political purposes." Yet, his public professions of Christian faith masked his warped, so-called "positive Christianity," which predictably was a religion of struggle and violence. Indeed, Hitler's Jesus was a "whip-wielding" Aryan who fought against "Jewish materialism." And his St. Paul was a "sneaky first-century rabbi" who "corrupted the teachings of Jesus." Hitler's long-tem goal was to abolish the Christian churches in Germany, but he opted for an incremental approach of control by increasing restrictions. In this, he was convinced that Christianity would "slowly fade away" as science rendered its teachings absurd.

Some have viewed Hitler as an occultist or a paganist. No doubt, a few high-ranking Nazis—most notably Heinrich Himmler—leaned in those directions. But Weikart provides evidence that Hitler's attitude toward both was "generally negative."

After narrowing the range of Hitler's religious options, Weikart candidly notes that reasonable cases can be made for other alternatives—agnosticism, deism, and non-Christian theism. However, in the final analysis, he concludes Hitler was most likely a "scientific pantheist," one who stressed the determinism of natural laws. There is considerable evidence that Hitler equated eternal nature with God, "ascribing a will and actions to nature that are normally reserved for a deity." Since nature, for Hitler, was the source of moral law, it is not surprising that he viewed "nature as justification for his violent policies." Complicating the matter of Hitler's pantheism was the fact that the dictator's private religious convictions were often tempered by political expediency. He was politically

THE RISE OF ADOLF HITLER

savvy enough to recognize the need for popular support of his regime, especially during the war years. Thus, he would invoke the Almighty, Divine Providence, and the Creator and resort to some traditional religious terminology in his public pronouncements, while in private defining them in non-traditional ways. None of this, according to Weikart, alters the strongly likelihood that Hitler was a pantheist.

Building on his earlier work on Nazism and evolutionary ethics, Weikart concludes his book with two chapters dedicated to some of the chilling implications of Hitler's religion. The dictator subscribed to an aggressive, Aryan-oriented social Darwinist position whereby anything that advanced the Nordic race was morally good and whatever led to biological degeneration was reprehensible. This translated into a "pitiless vision of the world" where "fighting in the struggle for existence was an ethical imperative with divine sanction." Things like "cruelty, oppression, murder, and even genocide were [therefore] morally justified, in his view, if they advanced the cause of the German Volk. Hitler cultivated a heartless conscience "that did not care if some people were exterminated in the global struggle for existence." His so-called religion justified "uninterrupted killing, so that the better [read Aryan and German in particular] will live."

Weikart performs a great service in sorting through all of the evidence, providing clarity to a contentious debate, and pointing readers towards Hitler's pantheism. His approach of eliminating possible religious options is a reasonable way to proceed, but it does lead to fair amount of overlap and repetition.

Surely, Hitler was a demonic, hate-filled opportunist. The Hitler that emerges from Weikart's pages, moreover, was a freethinking pantheist who coldly embraced the harsh logic of a twisted set of beliefs. And those beliefs, we all know, had utterly horrific consequences.

(Donald A. Yerxa is editor of Fides et Historia and professor of history emeritus at Eastern Nazarene College.)

Chapter – 13

Speeches of Adolf Hitler

1. Speech on the Treaty of Versailles (April 17, 1923) - Adolf Hitler

With the armistice begins the humiliation of Germany. If the Republic on the day of its foundation had appealed to the country: Germans, stand together! Up and resist the foe! The Fatherland, the Republic expects of you that you fight to your last breath, then millions who are now enemies of the Republic would be fanatical Republicans. Today they are the foes of the Republic not because it is a Republic but because this Republic was founded at the moment when Germany was humiliated, because it so discredited the new flag that men's eyes must turn regretfully toward the old flag.

So long as this Treaty stands there can be no resurrection of the German people; no social reform of any kind is possible! The Treaty was made in order to bring 20 million Germans to their deaths and to ruin the

German nation. But those who made the Treaty cannot set it aside. As its foundation our Movement formulated three demands:

1. Setting aside of the Peace Treaty.

2. Unification of all Germans.

3. Land and soil [Grund und Boden] to feed our nation.

Our movement could formulate these demands, since it was not our Movement which caused the War, it has not made the Republic, it did not sign the Peace Treaty.

There is thus one thing which is the first task of this Movement: it desires to make the German once more National, that his Fatherland shall stand for him above everything else. It desires to teach our

people to understand afresh the truth of the old saying: He who will not be a hammer must be an anvil.

An anvil we are today, and that anvil will be beaten until out of the anvil we fashion once more a hammer, a German sword!

Note: Text of speech from Aspects of Western Civilization, Volume II, Perry Rogers, ed.; Prentice Hall (2000)

2.   The Rise of Hitler: the Hammer or the Anvil (Excerpt of a speech given by Adolf Hitler in Munich on March 15, 1929)

"The entire struggle for survival is a conquest of the means of existence, which in turn results in the elimination of others from these same sources of subsistence. As long as there are people on this earth, there will be nations against nations and they will be forced to protect their vital rights …

One is either the hammer or the anvil. We confess it is our purpose to prepare the German people for the role of the hammer. For ten years we have preached, and our deepest concern is: How can we achieve power? We admit freely and openly that if our movement is victorious, we will be concerned day and night with the question of how to produce the armed forces which are forbidden to us by the peace treaty (Treaty of Versailles). We solemnly confess that we consider everyone a scoundrel who does not try day and night to figure out a way to violate this treaty, for we have never recognized this treaty.

We will take every step which strengthens our arms, which augments the number of our forces, and which increases the strength of our people.

We confess further that we will dash anyone to pieces who should dare to hinder us in this undertaking ... Our rights will never be represented by others. Our rights will be protected only when the German Reich is again supported by the point of the German dagger."

3. January 30, 1939 Reichstag Speech

Amid rising international tensions Führer and Reich Chancellor Adolf Hitler tells the German public and the world that the outbreak of war would mean the end of European Jewry—the "annihilation of the Jewish race in Europe."

Inspired by Hitler's theories of racial struggle and the supposed "intent" of the Jews to survive and expand at the expense of Germans, the Nazis ordered anti-Jewish boycotts, staged book burnings, and enacted anti-Jewish legislation. But it was the nationwide pogroms (Kristallnacht) in 1938 and the outbreak of war in 1939 that marked the transition in Nazi racial antisemitism toward genocide.

To justify the murder of the Jews both to the perpetrators and to bystanders in Germany and Europe, the Nazis used not only racist arguments but also arguments derived from older negative stereotypes, including Jews as communist subversives, as war profiteers and hoarders, and as a danger to internal security because of their inherent disloyalty and opposition to Germany.

4. Adolf Hitler: The Obersalzberg Speech, 22 Aug 1939

Decision to attack Poland was arrived at in spring. Originally there was fear that because of the political constellation we would have to strike at the same time against England, France, Russia and Poland. This risk too we should have had to take. Goring had demonstrated to us that his Four-Year Plan is a failure and that we are at the end of our strength, if we do not achieve victory in a coming war.

Since the autumn of 1938 and since I have realised that Japan will not go with us unconditionally and that Mussolini is endangered by that nitwit of a King and the treacherous scoundrel of a Crown Prince, I decided to go with Stalin. After all there are only three great statesmen in the world, Stalin, I and Mussolini. Mussolini is the weakest, for he has been able to break the power neither of the crown nor of the Church. Stalin and 1 are the only ones who visualise the future. So in a few weeks hence I shall stretch out my hand to Stalin at the common German-Russian frontier and with him undertake to re-distribute the world.

Our strength lies in our quickness and in our brutality; Genghis Khan has sent millions of women and children into death knowingly and with a light heart. History sees in him only the great founder of States. As to what the weak Western European civilisation asserts about me, that is of no account. I have given the command and I shall shoot everyone who utters one word of criticism, for the goal to be obtained in the war is not that of reaching certain lines but of physically demolishing the opponent. And so for the present only in the East 1 have put my death-head formations' in place with the command relentlessly and without compassion to send into death many women and children of Polish origin and language. Only thus we can gain the living space [lebensraum] that we need. Who after all is today speaking about the destruction of the Armenians?

Colonel-General von Brauchitsch has promised me to bring the war against Poland to a close within a few weeks. Had he reported to me that he needs two years or even only one year, I should not have given the command to march and should have allied myself temporarily with England instead of Russia for we cannot conduct a long war. To be sure a new situation has arisen. I experienced those poor worms Daladier and Chamberlain in Munich. They will be too cowardly to attack. They won't go beyond a blockade. Against that we have our autarchy and the Russian raw materials.

Poland will be depopulated and settled with Germans. My pact with the Poles was merely conceived of as a gaining of time. As for the rest, gentlemen, the fate of Russia will be exactly the same as 1 am now going through with in the case of Poland. After Stalin's death-he is a very sick man-we will break the Soviet Union. Then there will begin the dawn of the German rule of the earth.

The little States cannot scare me. After Kemal's [i.e. Ataturk] death Turkey is governed by cretins and half idiots. Carol of Roumania is through and through the corrupt slave of his sexual instincts. The King of Belgium and the Nordic kings are soft jumping jacks who are dependent upon the good digestions of their over-eating and tired peoples.

We shall have to take into the bargain the defection of Japan. I save Japan a full year's time. The Emperor is a counterpart to the last Czar - weak, cowardly, undecided. May he become a victim of the revolution. My going together with Japan never was popular. We shall continue to create disturbances in the Far East and in Arabia. Let us think as "gentlemen" and let us see in these peoples at best lacquered half maniacs who are anxious to experience the whip.

The opportunity is as favourable as never before. 1 have but one worry, namely that Chamberlain or some other such pig of a fellow (Saukerl) will come at the last moment with proposals or with ratting (Umfall). He will fly down the stairs, even if I shall personally have to trample on his belly in the eyes of the photographers.

No, it is too late for this. The attack upon and the destruction of Poland begins Saturday early. 1 shall let a few companies in Polish uniform attack in Upper Silesia or in the Protectorate. Whether the world believes it is quite indifferent (scheissegal). The world believes only in success.

For you, gentlemen, fame and honour are beginning as they have not since centuries. Be hard, be without mercy, act more quickly and brutally than the others. The citizens of Western Europe must tremble with horror. That is the most human way of conducting a war. For it scares the others off.

The new method of conducting war corresponds to the new drawing of the frontiers. A war extending from Reval, Lublin, Kaschau to the mouth of the Danube. The rest will be given to the Russians. Ribbentrop has orders to make every offer and to accept every demand. In the West I reserve to myself the right to determine the strategically best line. Here one will be able to work with Protectorate regions, such as Holland, Belgium and French Lorraine.

And now, on to the enemy, in Warsaw we will celebrate our reunion.

The speech was received with enthusiasm. Göring jumped on a table, thanked blood-thirstily and made blood-thirsty promises. He danced like a wild man. The few that had misgivings remained quiet.

Source: From Documents on British Foreign Policy. 1919-1939. eds. E. L. Woodward and Rohan Riftlep; 3rd series (London: HMSO, 1954), 7:258-260.

   THE RISE OF ADOLF HITLER

5. Hitler's Speech to the Commanders in Chief (August 22, 1939)

On May 23, 1939, just a day after signing the "Pact of Steel", Hitler told his generals that a German invasion of Poland was now inevitable. The conflict over Danzig and the Polish corridor was mere pretext. Germany could simply no longer do without Eastern European "living space" [Lebensraum] and the attendant raw materials. Hitler therefore declared his willingness to accept the possibility of a declaration of war by England and France. His greatest concern was a possible Soviet intervention on the side of the western Allies. But when, on August 21, 1939, he received Stalin's agreement to enter into a German-Soviet pact, Hitler saw that the course had been set for war. (Reich Foreign Minister Joachim von Ribbentrop and Soviet Foreign Minister Vyacheslav Molotov signed the pact two days later in Moscow.) On August 22, 1939, Hitler invited his generals to yet another situation meeting. On September 1, 1939, the invasion of Poland began.

Speech by the Führer to the Commanders in Chief on August 22, 1939

"I have called you together to give you a picture of the political situation, in order that you may have some insight into the individual factors on which I have based my decision to act and in order to strengthen your confidence.

After this we shall discuss military details.

It was clear to me that a conflict with Poland had to come sooner or later. I had already made this decision in the spring, but I thought that I would first turn against the West in a few years, and only after that against the East. But the sequence of these things cannot be fixed. Nor should one close one's eyes to threatening situations. I wanted first of all to establish a tolerable relationship with Poland in order to fight first against the West. But this plan, which appealed to me, could not be executed, as fundamental points had changed. It became clear to me that, in the event of a conflict with the West, Poland would attack us. Poland is striving for access to the sea. The further development appeared after the occupation of the Memel Territory and it became clear to me that in certain circumstances a conflict with Poland might come at an inopportune moment. I give as reasons for this conclusion:

1. First of all two personal factors:

My own personality and that of Mussolini.

Essentially all depends on me, on my existence, because of my political talents. Furthermore, the fact that probably no one will ever again have the trust of the whole German people as I have. There will probably never again in the future be a man with more authority than I have. My existence is therefore a factor of great value. But I can be eliminated at any time by a criminal or a lunatic.

The second personal factor is the Duce. His existence is also decisive. If anything happens to him, Italy's loyalty to the alliance will no longer be certain. The Italian Court is fundamentally opposed to the Duce. Above all, the Court regards the expansion of the empire as an encumbrance. The Duce is the man with the strongest nerves in Italy.

The third personal factor in our favour is Franco. We can ask only for benevolent neutrality from Spain. But this depends on Franco's personality. He guarantees a certain uniformity and stability in the present system in Spain. We must accept the fact that Spain does not as yet have a Fascist party with our internal unity.

The other side presents a negative picture as far as authoritative persons are concerned. There is no outstanding personality in England and France.

It is easy for us to make decisions. We have nothing to lose; we have everything to gain. Because of our restrictions [Einschränkungen] our economic situation is such that we can only hold out for a few more years. Göring can confirm this. We have no other choice, we must act. Our opponents will be risking a great deal and can gain only a little. Britain's stake in a war is inconceivably great. Our enemies have leaders who are below the average. No personalities. No masters, no men of action.

Besides the personal factors, the political situation is favorable for us: In the Mediterranean, rivalry between Italy, France and England; in the Far East, tension between Japan and England; in the Middle East, tension which causes alarm in the Mohammedan world."

6.   Speech at Nuremberg, September 14, 1935 at Hitler Youth rally

Nothing is possible unless one will commands, a will which has to be obeyed by others, beginning at the top and ending only at the very bottom. This is the expression of an authoritarian state – not of a weak, babbling democracy – of an authoritarian state where everyone is proud to obey, because he knows: I will likewise be obeyed when I must take command.

7.   Speech in Austria, April 9, 1938 German voters

To justify the annexation of Austria, Hitler called for a public vote on whether the unification should stand. This is an excerpt from a speech he gave on April 9, 1938, the day before the vote. As Hitler points out in his speech, he himself was born, and grew up, in Austria.

When one day we shall be no more, then the coming generations shall be able to look back with pride upon this day, the day on which a great Volk affirmed the German community. In the past, millions of German men shed their blood for this Reich. How merciful a fate to be allowed to create this Reich today without a suffering. Now, rise, German Volk, subscribe to it, hold it tightly in your hands! I wish to thank Him who allowed me to return to my homeland so that I could return it to my German Reich! May every German realize the importance of the hour tomorrow, assess it and then bow his head in reverence before the will of the Almighty who has wrought this miracle in all of us within these past few weeks.

Chapter - 14

Eva Braun: Life with Adolf Hitler

Eva Anna Paula Hitler was a German photographer who was a longtime companion and wife of Adolf Hitler. Braun met Hitler in Munich when she was a 17-year-old assistant and model for Heinrich Hoffmann. She began seeing Hitler often about two years later.

She attempted suicide twice during their early relationship. By 1936, Braun was a part of Hitler's household at the Berghof near Berchtesgaden, Bavaria, Germany, and lived a sheltered life throughout World War II. She became a significant figure within Hitler's inner social circle, but did not attend public events with him until mid-1944, when her sister Gretl married Hermann Fegelein, the SS liaison officer on his staff.

As Nazi Germany was collapsing towards the end of the war, Braun swore loyalty to Hitler and went to Berlin to be by his side in the heavily reinforced Führerbunker beneath the Reich Chancellery garden. As Red Army troops fought their way into the centre government district, on 29th April 1945, Braun married Hitler during a brief civil ceremony. At that time she was 33 and he was 56. Less than forty hours later, they died by suicide in a sitting room of the bunker: Braun by biting and swallowing a capsule of cyanide, and Hitler by a gunshot on his head. The German public was unaware of Braun's relationship with Hitler until after their death. Many of the surviving colour photographs and films of Hitler were taken by Braun.

Early Life

Eva Braun was born in Munich and was the second daughter of Friedrich "Fritz" Braun (1879–1964)[1] and Franziska "Fanny" Kronberger (1885–1976. She had an elder sister, Ilse (1909–1979), and a younger sister, Margarete (Gretl) (1915–1987). Her father was a Lutheran and her mother a Catholic.

Braun's parents were divorced in April 1921 but remarried in November 1922, probably for financial reasons. Braun was educated at a Catholic lyceum in Munich, and then for one year at a business school in the Convent of the English Sisters in Simbach am Inn, where she had average grades and a talent for athletics.

At the age of 17 years, Braun took a job under Heinrich Hoffmann, the official photographer for the Nazi Party. Initially employed as a shop assistant and sales clerk, she soon learned how to use a camera and develop photographs. She met Adolf Hitler, 23 years her senior, at Hoffmann's studio in Munich in October 1929. He had been introduced to her as "Herr Wolff". Braun's younger sister, Gretl, also worked for Hoffmann. Both rented an apartment together for a time. Gretl often accompanied Eva on her subsequent trips with Hitler to Obersalzberg.

Relationship with Hitler

Hitler lived with his half-niece, Geli Raubal, in an apartment at Prinzregentenplatz in Munich . On 18th September of that year, Raubal was found dead in the apartment with a gunshot wound to the chest, an apparent suicide with Hitler's pistol. Hitler was in Nuremberg at that time. His relationship with Raubal—likely the most intense of his life—had been important to him. Hitler began seeing more of Braun after Raubal's suicide.

Braun herself attempted suicide on 10th August 1932 by shooting herself in the chest with her father's pistol. Historians feel the attempt was not serious, but was a bid for Hitler's attention. After Braun's recovery, Hitler became more committed to her. She often stayed overnight at his

Munich apartment when he was in town. Beginning in 1933, Braun worked as a photographer for Hoffmann. This position enabled her to travel—accompanied by Hoffmann—with Hitler's entourage as a photographer for the Nazi Party. Later in her career, she worked for Hoffmann's art press.

According to a fragment of her diary and the account of biographer Nerin Gun, Braun's second suicide attempt occurred in May 1935. She took an overdose of sleeping pills when Hitler failed to make time for her in his life. Hitler provided Braun and her sister with a three-bedroom apartment in Munich that August, and the next year the sisters were provided with a villa in Bogenhausen at Wasserburgerstr. 12. By 1936, Braun was at Hitler's household at the Berghof near Berchtesgaden whenever he was in residence there, but she lived mostly in Munich. Braun also had her own apartment at the new Reich Chancellery in Berlin, completed to a design by Albert Speer.

Braun was a member of Hoffmann's staff when she attended the Nuremberg Rally for the first time in 1935. Hitler's half-sister, Angela Raubal (Geli's mother), took exception to her presence there and was later dismissed from her position as housekeeper at the Berghof. Researchers are unable to ascertain if her dislike for Braun was the only reason for her departure, but other members of Hitler's entourage saw Braun as untouchable from then on.

Hitler wished to present himself in the image of a chaste hero; in the Nazi ideology, men were the political leaders and warriors, and women were homemakers. Hitler believed that he was sexually attractive to women and wished to exploit this for political gain by remaining single, as he felt marriage would decrease his appeal. He and Braun never appeared as a couple in public; the only time they appeared together in a published news photo was when she sat near him at the 1936 Winter Olympics. The German people were unaware of Braun's relationship with Hitler until after the war. Braun had her own room adjoining Hitler's at both the Berghof and the Führerbunker complex beneath the Reich Chancellery garden in Berlin.

Braun's political influence on Hitler was minimal; she was never allowed to stay in the room when business or political conversations took place and was sent out of the room when cabinet ministers or other dignitaries were present. She was not a member of the Nazi Party. In his post-war memoirs, Hoffmann characterized Braun's outlook as "inconsequential and feather-brained"; her main interests were sports, clothes, and the cinema. She led a sheltered and privileged existence and seemed uninterested in politics. One instance when she took an interest was in 1943, shortly after Germany had fully transitioned to a total war economy; among other things, this meant a potential ban on women's cosmetics and luxuries. According to Speer's memoirs, Braun approached Hitler in "high indignation"; Hitler quietly instructed Speer, who was armaments minister at the time, to halt production of women's cosmetics and luxuries rather than instituting an outright ban. Speer later said, "Eva Braun will prove a great disappointment to historians."

Braun continued to work for Hoffmann after commencing her relationship with Hitler. She took many photographs and films of members of Hitler's inner circle, some of which were sold to Hoffmann for extremely high prices; she received money from Hoffmann's company as late as 1943. Braun also held the position of private secretary to Hitler. This guise meant she could enter and leave the Chancellery unremarked, though she used a side entrance and a rear staircase. Görtemaker notes that Braun and Hitler enjoyed a normal sex life. Braun's friends and relatives described Eva giggling over a 1938 photograph of Neville Chamberlain sitting on a sofa in Hitler's Munich flat with the remark: "If only he knew what goings-on that sofa has seen."

On 3rd June 1944, Braun's sister Gretl married SS-Gruppenführer Hermann Fegelein, who served as Reichsführer-SS Heinrich Himmler's liaison officer on Hitler's staff. Hitler used the marriage as an excuse to allow Braun to appear at official functions, as she could then be introduced as Fegelein's sister-in-law. When Fegelein was caught in the closing days of the war trying to escape to Sweden or Switzerland, Hitler ordered his execution. He was shot for desertion in the garden of the Reich Chancellery on 28th April 1945.

Lifestyle

When Hitler purchased the Berghof in 1933, it was a small holiday home on the mountain at Obersalzberg. Renovations began in 1934 and were completed by 1936. A large wing was added onto the original house and several additional buildings were constructed. The entire area was fenced off, and remaining houses on the mountain were purchased by the Nazi Party and demolished. Braun and the other members of the entourage were cut off from the outside world when in residence. Speer, Hermann Göring, and Martin Bormann had houses constructed inside the compound.

Hitler's valet, Heinz Linge, stated in his memoirs that Hitler and Braun had two bedrooms and two bathrooms with interconnecting doors at the Berghof, and Hitler would end most evenings alone with her in his study before they retired to bed. She would wear a "dressing gown or house-coat" and drink wine; Hitler would have tea. Public displays of affection or physical contact were nonexistent, even in the enclosed world of the Berghof. Braun took the role of hostess amongst the regular visitors, though she was not involved in running the household. She regularly invited friends and family members to accompany her during her stays, the only guest to do so.

When Henriette von Schirach suggested that Braun should go into hiding after the war, Braun replied, "Do you think I would let him die alone? I will stay with him up until the last moment". Hitler named Braun in his will, to receive 12,000 Reichsmarks yearly after his death. He was very fond of her, and worried when she participated in sports or was late returning for tea.

Braun was very fond of Negus and Stasi, her two Scottish Terrier dogs. She usually kept them away from Hitler's German Shepherd, Blondi. Blondi was killed by one of Hitler's entourage on 29th April 1945 when he ordered that one of the cyanide capsules obtained for Braun and Hitler's suicide the next day be tested on the dog. Braun's dogs and Blondi's puppies were shot on 30 April by Hitler's dog handler, Fritz Tornow.

Marriage and Suicide

In early April 1945, Braun travelled from Munich to Berlin to be with Hitler at the Führerbunker. She refused to leave as the Red Army closed in on the capital. After midnight on the night of 28–29th April, Hitler and Braun were married in a small civil ceremony within the bunker. The event was witnessed by Joseph Goebbels and Martin Bormann. Thereafter, Hitler hosted a modest wedding breakfast with his new wife. When Braun married Hitler, her legal name changed to Eva Hitler. When she signed her marriage certificate, she wrote the letter B for her family name, then crossed this out and replaced it with Hitler.

After 1:00 pm on 30th April 1945, Braun and Hitler said their farewell to staff and members of the inner circle. Later that afternoon, at approximately 3:30 pm, several people reported hearing a loud gunshot. After waiting a few minutes, Linge, accompanied by Hitler's SS adjutant, Otto Günsche, entered the small study and found the lifeless bodies of Hitler and Braun on a small sofa. Braun had bitten into a cyanide capsule, and Hitler had shot himself in the right temple with his pistol. The corpses were carried up the stairs and through the bunker's emergency exit to the garden behind the Reich Chancellery, where they were burned during the Red Army shelling in and around the area. Braun was 33 years old when she died and Adolf Hitler was 56.

By 11th May, Hitler's dentist's assistant Käthe Heusermann and dental technician Fritz Echtmann identified dental remains as belonging to Hitler and Braun. The remains of Joseph and Magda Goebbels, the six Goebbels children, General Hans Krebs, and Hitler's dogs were repeatedly buried and exhumed, with the last location being the SMERSH compound in Magdeburg, East Germany. Hitler and Braun's remains were alleged to have been moved as well, but this is most likely Soviet disinformation. There is no evidence that any bodily remains of Hitler or Braun – with the exception of the dental remains – were found by the Soviets. On 4th April 1970, a Soviet KGB team with detailed burial charts secretly exhumed five wooden boxes of remains in Magdeburg. The remains were thoroughly burned and crushed, after which the ashes were thrown into the Biederitz river, a tributary of the nearby Elbe.

The rest of Braun's family survived the war. Her mother, Franziska, died at age 91 in January 1976, having lived out her days in an old farmhouse in Ruhpolding, Bavaria. Her father, Fritz, died in 1964. Gretl gave birth to a daughter—whom she named Eva—on 5th May 1945. She later married Kurt Beringhoff, a businessman. She died in 1987. Braun's elder sister, Ilse, was not part of Hitler's inner circle. She married twice and died in 1979.

Chapter – 15

As in Life so in Death: Hubris and Delusion defined Adolf Hitler

A little after midnight on April 28/29, 1945, Adolf Hitler asked his secretary Gertraud Junge to help him with some paperwork.

Junge happened to be one of the two secretaries working for Hitler in the last few weeks of his life; Gerda Christian being the other. Joseph Goebbels with his wife and six children, Martin Bormann, Nicholas von Below (Hitler's adjutant) and Generals Hans Krebs and Wilhelm Burgdorf made up the rest of the Fuehrer's entourage. Besides, of course, Eva Braun, whom Hitler had married just a little while earlier that night in a modest civil wedding, where a junior functionary of the Berlin city administration, pulled out from his Nazi guard duty, officiated as the marriage registrar.

The wedding breakfast was in progress in a large room inside the Fuehrerbunker, champagne bottles were being uncorked, and everyone was congratulating the newly-married couple when Hitler motioned to Junge to follow him into one of his workrooms on the same floor. The Red Army was within whistling distance of Hitler's last refuge. Relentless artillery fire was pounding the Reich Chancellery garden above, but 50 feet inside the ground, the formidable bunker fortifications held up quite well still.

Hitler told Junge that he was going to dictate his political and personal testaments, which he would leave behind for posterity's sake. He had already made it known that he would kill himself before the Russians got to him, so the young secretary, always in awe of the Fuehrer, "sat in nervous excitement, expecting to hear a profound explanation of the great sacrifice's true purpose."

Hitler then proceeded to spell out first **My Personal Will** and **My Political Statement**. He kept referring to some notes and documents he had with him, presumably provided by Goebbels, but the whole thing took quite some time. By the time the typing was done, the documents signed and Hitler's seal affixed to the documents in presence of witnesses, it was a little after 4 a.m. on April 29.

Goebbels, Bormann, Burgdoff and Krebs set their hands as witnesses to the political testament while Bormann and Nicholas von Below did the honours for the Fuehrer's personal will. Bormann ('my most faithful Party comrade') was named as the executor of the will. Hitler was to die about 36 hours later (on April 30), the Goebbels's on the following day, and Bormann the day after.

Unlike the others who took their own lives (the Goebbels children having been poisoned by their parents), Bormann probably died while fleeing the Red Army outside Berlin.

Hitler's will

Hitler's last will and testament are fascinating documents for a variety of reasons, though they do not appear to have received even a fraction of the attention that **'Mein Kampf'** always did, or does even today.

This is surprising, given that we usually believe a man is apt to reveal a lot about himself when taking leave of life. Indeed, Hitler's 'swan song' throws more light on the man than ten learned biographies could have hoped to do together. And it does so with the panache we associate with Hitler in the full panoply of his powers.

So, it should be worthwhile going over these two statements briefly today.

The 'will' is a short document of about 275 words, and it touches upon three things: Hitler's decision to marry Eva Braun just before they were to die; how his personal effects were to be disposed of; and his resolve to die (with his newly-wedded wife) at the precise place from where he rendered '12 years' service to my people'. It contains the appropriately grand statement that:

"What I possess belongs – in so far as it has any value – to the Party. Should this no longer exist, to the State; should the State also be destroyed, no further decision is necessary."

The most significant part of the will refers to Eva Braun, Hitler's mistress of many years, whom the Fuehrer formally recognised as his companion just a day before her death. Before that, for nearly 14 years, Eva was there but yet not quite there. She lived in the Reich's shadows, never allowed to take part in official ceremonies or banquets.

Twice, she attempted suicide – apparently in the hope that Hitler would give his long-time lover her due – but the Fuehrer had very different ideas on the subject. He was to be the messiah, Germany's guardian angel, chaste and celibate, untouched by the temptations of the flesh. So how could he attest to his own susceptibility to the charms of an ordinary woman, however pretty and dainty? (It has also been suggested that, till the very end, Hitler relished the idea of his being irresistibly attractive to the entire feminine half of Germany as the nation's most eligible bachelor.)

In his will, Hitler recognises the 'many years of true friendship' that Eva had given him, also that she chose, 'of her own free will', to be by his side till the bitter end (even though she had been offered other options). But, incredibly, he does not once name her. So, the 33-year-old Braun is simply referred to by her 56-year-old lover as 'the woman', thus to remain as anonymous in death as she had been for much of her life.

Instead, Hitler waxes eloquent on how 'during the long years of struggle (he) believed that (he) could not undertake the responsibility of marriage', but that, 'before the end of (his) life', he had decided to make this grand gesture of legitimising his relationship with a devoted soul. Even in his dying hour, the megalomaniac remained as manically self-absorbed as ever.

Hitler's political testament

Hitler's political testament, split in two parts, is a more elaborate affair. The first part is a recapitulation of his **weltanschaung** set out in the specific context of his years as the helmsman of the Reich. The second section addresses the question of succession in the Nazi leadership after him.

In this section, he also vents his ire on two former aides, Hermann Goering and Heinrich Himmler who, he says, had abused his trust and thus merited the denunciation (and expulsion from the Nazi leadership) which he sets down in his testament.

After invoking his 'modest contribution as a volunteer in the first world war', Hitler quickly moves to his main thesis, which is that neither he 'nor anybody else in Germany wanted war in 1939'.

Indeed, Hitler himself 'made too many offers of limitation and control of armaments' for the responsibility of World War 11 to be laid at his door. But all went in vain, because 'International Jewry and its helpers' were hell-bent on forcing the war upon Germany. A mere three days before Germany's invasion of Poland, Hitler had 'again proposed to the British ambassador in Berlin a solution to the German-Polish problem', but 'partly under influence of propaganda by International Jewry', Britain failed to act on that excellent suggestion.

After this, Hitler launched into a spirited defence of what he was 'obliged' to resort to in course of a war he presumably never wanted to wage: "I also made it quite plain (before the hostilities began) that if the peoples of Europe were again to be regarded merely as pawns in the game played by the international conspiracy of money and finance, then the Jews, the race which is the real guilty party in this murderous struggle, would be saddled with the responsibility for it. I left no one in doubt that this time not only would millions of children of the European Aryan races starve, not only would millions of grown men meet their death and not only would hundreds of thousands of women and children be burnt and bombed to death in the cities, but this time the real culprits would have to pay for their guilt, even though by more humane means than war."

It is difficult to find a clearer statement of intent in all of recorded history. Hitler had, he says, put everyone on notice what they were to expect from him, and he could not now be faulted for being true to his word.

The Holocaust was the only sensible –and civilised – response to the onslaught on the 'European Aryan races' (unleashed by the 'International Jewry'), and Hitler could not but have exercised that option. Come to think of it, wasn't gassing men, women and children to death a 'more humane means than war'?

Here was a man whose many delusions (of 'the pure race', the thousand-year Reich, of Germany being perpetually under attack from the Jews and the Slavs…) precipitated the most catastrophic war in history, a war that claimed no fewer than 85 million human lives. Over 55% of all European Jews were murdered, with countries like Poland, the Netherlands, Greece and Yugoslavia losing over 90% of their Jewish populations.

The Soviet Union lost to the war one in every seven citizens (one of her constituent republics, Belarus, lost one in every four) and Hitler's own Germany one in 12. And yet we have this extraordinary spectacle of the hangman calmly musing over his macabre exploits! Remorse is the furthest from his heart. He has never known horror, except the horror of possible defeat. He is not merely unrepentant: he grieves that he did not do enough harm.

"The world fell asleep, as that world awoke," Karl Kraus had said about the world of national socialism. It's not hard to see what Kraus meant.

As his make-believe world crumbled all around him, Hitler yet clung tenaciously to his ludicrous fantasies: "I die with a joyful heart in my knowledge of the immeasurable deeds and achievements of our soldiers at the front, of our women at home, of our peasants and workers and of the contribution, unique in history, of our youth which bears my name… (It's my) wish that they should therefore not give up the struggle under any circumstances, but carry it on wherever they may be against the enemies of the fatherland…"

For perspective, of the eight million German deaths in World War 11, more than half were accounted for by the war's last seven months, when even the most die-hard Nazi fanatic knew that the game was up, that countless civilian lives were to be sacrificed unless Hitler ended his insane campaign.

Indeed, even after Berlin was taken by the Red Army on May 1/2, SS officers paid homage to their Fuehrer by summarily executing civilians who happened to put up the white flag of surrender to the rampaging Russians.

The brutalised, utterly dehumanised culture of superiority that Hitler so assiduously cultivated in his men scarred the souls of many, maybe most, ordinary Germans as well.

Even in death, Hitler was as hubris-ridden as he was at the pinnacle of his power. While expelling Goering (whom, by a June 1941 decree, Hitler

 THE RISE OF ADOLF HITLER

had named as his successor) and Himmler for their suspected treachery, he could not help the typical fuehreresque flourish.

Told that Himmler was negotiating with the Allies for surrender, Hitler had Hermann Fegelein, a close aide of Himmler's and at the time part of Hitler's personal staff, executed on April 28.

Fegelein was married to Gretl, Eva Braun's sister, who was heavily pregnant at that point. Eva pleaded with Hitler for clemency. Hitler rebuffed her – and married her a few hours later. In his testament, with usual pompousness, he named the cabinet that would succeed him, regardless of the fact that it was to take office in the most surreal circumstances. And even in this, he made sure that there was to be no 'claimant' to his own status: he apportioned his powers to three of the most-faithful – Goebbels, Donitz and Bormann.

"Hitler clearly wanted to continue his policy of divide and rule from beyond the grave, even on the most spectral administration ever assembled," as historian Anthony Beevor noted.

Appropriately, Hitler's last call to his country, recorded in the concluding paragraph of his political testament, harked back to his greatest delusion:

Above all, I enjoin the government of the nation and the people to uphold the racial laws to the limit and to resist mercilessly the poisoner of all nations – International Jewry.

Chapter – 16

Quotes by Adolf Hitler – (1889-1945)

Adolf Hitler led the Nazi party from 1921 to 1945. He served as **Chancellor of Germany** from 1933 to 1945, and as dictatorial leader of the **Third Reich** from 1934 to 1945.

He initiated World War II with the invasion of Poland in September 1939 and played a vital role in the Holocaust.

Quotations

- How fortunate for governments that the people they administer don't think.

- For the sake of historical truth I must verify that only the Greeks, of all the adversaries who confronted us, fought with bold courage and highest disregard of death. (speech before the Reichstag, 4th May 1941)

- If you win, you need not have to explain...If you lose, you should not be there to explain!

- To conquer a nation, first disarm its citizens.

- Do not compare yourself to others. If you do so, you are insulting yourself.

- Anyone can deal with victory. Only the mighty can bear defeat.

- The victor will never be asked if he told the truth.

- If you want to shine like sun first you have to burn like it.

- You will never learn what I am thinking. And those who boast most loudly that they know my thought, to such people I lie even more.

- There is a better chance of seeing a camel pass through the eye of a needle than of seeing a really great man 'discovered' through an election.

- Winning without problem is just victory, but winning with lots of trouble create History.

- The god of war has gone over to the other side. (after Stalingrad)

- What Marxism, Leninism and Stalinism failed to accomplish, we shall be in a position to achieve.

- The peoples of Islam will always be closer to us than, for example, France.

- Everything about the behaviour of American society reveals that it's half Judaised, and the other half negrified.

- The great strength of the totalitarian state is that it forces those who fear it to imitate it.

- Conscience is a Jewish invention.

- Reading is not an end to itself, but a means to an end.

- I'm sure that Nero didn't set fire to Rome. It was the Christian-Bolsheviks who did that, just as the Commune set fire to Paris in 1871 and the Communists set fire to the Reichstag in 1932.

- The art of reading consists in remembering the essentials and forgetting non essentials.

Chapter – 17

Mind-Boggling Facts about Adolf Hitler

Adolf Hitler was responsible for 60 to 85 million deaths during WW II. His name brings murder, misery, warfare, holocaust and the attempted extermination of the Jews and other minorities. Hitler openly expressed his hatred of Jews in his book **'Mein Kampf'.** He warned everyone about his intention to drive the Jews and minorities from Germany's cultural, intellectual and cultural life.

Before invading Poland, Hitler gave example of Genghis Khan to his generals. He said that though Genghis Khan led millions of women and children to slaughter with pre-determination, history still considered him solely the founder of the Mongol state; not as a murderer.

As a result of the Holocaust, 6 million Jews in Nazi occupied Europe at that time and an additional 5 million non-Jewish people were killed. From 1941 to 1945, Jews and other racial, political and ethnic minorities in Europe were targeted and systematically murdered by the Nazi forces.

Hitler shaved part of his moustache because his full moustache killed him:

Hitler's toothbrush style moustache was not always like this. During WW I he had a full moustache. Soldiers in trenches were experiencing mustard-gas and other lethal gas attacks during the WW I and respiratory masks were provided to the combatants to keep out gas. But during gas attacks, Hitler could not create complete airlocks pulling his respiratory mask over his face due to his long moustache and he almost died due to presence of gas in his mask.

As a result, Hitler's supervisors ordered Hitler to remove his fancy moustache to facilitate the wearing of the gas masks. But instead, he trimmed it to the distinctive toothbrush shaped style.

Hitler was nominated for Nobel Peace Prize in 1939:

Stalin and Hitler were nominated for the Nobel peace prize, the most distinguished award given to people who work towards world peace. Stalin was nominated in 1945 and 1948 for his contribution to end the Second World War.

However, Hitler's nomination was supposed to be an irony and a joke. EGC Brandt, a member of the Swedish parliament nominated Adolf Hitler for the peace prize in 1939. His intention was to satirically criticize the Swedish government, but it was not well received and he was forced to withdraw the nomination.

Hitler proposed the "Museum of an Extinct Race":

Hitler wanted to exterminate the entire Jewish race. His Nazi regime oversaw the genocide of six-million Jews. However, he did not want to eliminate memory of the Jews completely.

He ordered to retain the paintings, artifacts and valuable belongings of any Jews murdered. He wanted to create a museum for the German 'Aryan race' to come and watch such artifacts. He wished to call it 'Museum of an Extinct Race'.

Hitler made laws against animal cruelty:

He followed a vegetarian diet. Moreover, at social events he sometimes narrated graphic accounts of animal slaughtering in an effort to discourage his dinner guests to eat meat. There was a dedicated greenhouse build near his home in Obersalzberg in Bavaria to ensure a constant supply of fresh vegetables and fruits for him throughout the war. There is a legend that Hitler put off meat when he was young as a result of witnessing an autopsy and became determined in protecting animal rights.

He helped implement wild animal, cattle and chickens protection laws and intended to reduce meat consumption by the Germans after the Second World War.

Hitler wanted to become a priest during his childhood:

Hitler was born to a practicing Catholic mother and an anti-clerical father. When Hitler was 8-years- old he used to sing in church choir and took singing lessons to improve his vocals. He even aspired to become a priest.

However, later he favored some aspects of Protestantism. According to a U.S. Strategic Services report, Hitler planned to destroy the influence of Christian churches in German held territories. His intention to eliminate Christianity indicates that he became an atheist to the very core.

Hitler never visited a single Concentration Camp:

Most of the 11 million Jews and other minorities killed during the Holocaust by Hitler's Nazi forces were murdered at the 1,200 Nazi concentration camps. The first Nazi concentration camp was established in Germany in 1933 immediately after Hitler became Chancellor of the party. The first camps were initially used to hold and torture union organizers and political opponents.

During WW II, these became the places where millions of ordinary people and so called 'racially undesirable' minorities were enslaved, used as forced labor in the war industries, tortured and then brutally murdered in mass numbers.

Hitler never visited a single death camp. The distance Hitler kept between himself and the spot of actual killing has fueled the claims made by the neo-Nazi supporters that Hitler was not responsible for the holocaust and that Himmler kept him in the dark about what was taking place. However, Hitler's involvement in the genocide can be found at every stage of the 'Final Solution', a program aimed at murdering every last Jew within German controlled territories.

Hitler was selected Time Magazine's, Man of the Year for 1938:

Hitler, Chamberlain, French Prime Minister Édouard Daladier and Mussolini attended a one-day conference in Munich on September 29th 1938. British Prime Minister Neville Chamberlain appeased Hitler and convinced British and French politicians to accept some of Hitler's territorial claims in exchange for the assurance of no further aggression from Germany in an agreement called the **'Munich Agreement'**. As Germany had been granted the German speaking Sudetenland region of Czechoslovakia as per the agreement, it was perceived at that time to be a successful preventive measure against a possible outbreak of a world war. Due to the Munich summit, Hitler was selected **'Man of the Year'** by Times Magazine for 1938, a premature attribution beyond doubts.

Hitler had Parkinson's Disease:

Researchers have suggested that Hitler suffered from a number of diseases including Parkinson's disease. Some described him as a neurotic psychopath.

It is reported that for the last 11 years of his life, Hitler suffered from mental and physical symptoms of the Parkinson's disease. Some historians argued that his decision-making was affected during WW II due to his possible dementia or memory loss as a result of the disease.

One of Hitler's hobbies was whistling 'When You Wish Upon A Star':

Hitler reportedly relaxed by whistling tunes including 'when you wish upon a star'. He entertained dinner guests by whistling and performed the hobby in moments of euphoria - such as following the fall of Paris in June 1940.

'Who's Afraid of the Big Bad Wolf' was also one of his favorite tunes due to 'The Wolf' being his nickname. When the Germans had started to retreat from Russia, Hitler became forgetful and preoccupied. During that time, once he was whistling even while eating.

Hitler was temporarily blinded in a Gas Attack:

Hitler was temporarily blinded in a mustard gas attack in his camp on October 15th 1918 during the WW I. He was hospitalized in Pasewalk in

Germany. And while there, he learned of Germany's defeat and Armistice with Britain and France. He reportedly said that he had suffered a 'second temporary blindness' upon hearing such horrifying news for the Germans.

For Seven Years, Hitler Was 'Nationless':

Hitler later stated his goal for a **Großdeutschland** (Greater Germany). However, he was an Austrian by birth. From a young age, he longed to be a part of the German empire and despised the Austro-Hungarian empire and its Habsburg monarchy. He had formally renounced his Austrian citizenship in April, 1925 but did not obtain German citizenship immediately. He became stateless, faced the risk of deportation and was unable to run for public office.

Interior minister of Brunswick state in Germany was a member of the NSDAP or Nazi party. He appointed fellow party member Hitler as an administrator for the state in February 1932. Thus Hitler became a citizen of Brunswick and thus of Germany. He had been stateless for almost seven years.

Hitler's original Family Name was Schicklgruber:

Hitler's father Alois Hitler was the illegitimate child of Maria Anna Schicklgruber. Alois was born in 1837 but the baptismal register did not show his father's name. So, initially, Alois bore his mother's surname, Schicklgruber. Johann Georg Hiedler married Maria Anna in 1842.

Maria Anna died in 1847 and Alois changed his baptismal register in 1876 by recording Georg Hitler (Johann Georg Hiedler) as his father. Thus he assumed the surname **Hitler** which is also spelled as Hiedler, Huettler or Hüttler. Hitler surname is presumably based on 'one who lives in a hut'.

Hitler was awarded the Iron Cross First Class:

According to historians, Hitler avoided joining the Austro-Hungarian army during WW I. He later claimed that the 'mixture of races' in the Austro-Hungarian army was the reason behind his decision. He was living in Munich at the outbreak of WW I and he joined the Bavarian Army as an Austrian citizen. He was posted to the **Bavarian Reserve Infantry Regiment 16** and served as a dispatch runner or messenger on the Western Front in Belgium and France. Nearly half of his time in the WW I, he was well behind the front lines. However, he participated in the First Battle of Ypres, Battle of Arras, Battle of the Somme, Battle of Passchendaele. Hitler was wounded during the Battle of the Somme.

Hitler discovered his love for Germany during the First World War. Due to his contribution in the war, he was awarded the **Iron Cross, Second Class** in 1914. Hitler's Jewish superior, Lieutenant Hugo Gutmann recommended him and Hitler was awarded Iron Cross First Class on August 4th 1918 despite being a member of the Gefreiter, the second lowest rank in German Army.

Hitler admired Protestant Reformer Martin Luther:

Protestant reformation was a religious division within Western Christianity that attempted to reform the Roman Catholic Church by criticizing its practices such as - selling of indulgences, Pope's authority over purgatory, the Catholic doctrine of the merits of the saints, etc. In Catholicism, purgatory is an intermediate state after death where people with 'less sufficient' level of holiness go to undergo purification. The **'Merits of saints'** is a Catholic belief that states that the merits of Jesus Christ, his faithful and the communion of saints can benefit others too. These reformations were initiated by Martin Luther, John Calvin and others. Lutherans and Calvinists are two major branches of Protestant Christianity. Lutheran Churches were mostly founded in Germany as Martin Luther was a German friar and he initiated the movement in the 16th century.

During his stay in the men's hostel, Hitler reportedly criticized the **Germanophobia** of the Catholic Church. He said that Catholic Church had spilled more blood than any other religion. Despite he was brought up as a Catholic during his childhood, he despised Christianity and especially the papacy. But he admired Luther.

Hitler had to live in homeless shelters:

Like many Austrians, Hitler began to get attracted to German nationalist ideas from an early age. His father died when Hitler was 14- years-old and subsequently, Hitler's performance at school dropped. Two years later he changed school and enrolled at a school in Steyr in Upper Austria. After giving a repeat, he passed the final school exams. His mother died of breast cancer at the age of 47 on December 21st 1907. At the age of 18-19, he was twice rejected admission into the **Fine Arts Academy** (in 1907 and 1908) as he was declared unfit for painting. While in Vienna, he tried to make a living out of selling his paintings. But due to lack of quality and resources, he ran out of money soon. Hitler kept moving from one place to another as his savings gradually diminished and his lifestyle deteriorated. In December 1909, he was half starved and freezing and had to live in homeless shelters in Vienna and whenever he sold a painting, he would occasionally spend the night in men's hostels. He then moved into a public dormitory for men in Vienna and lived there for 3 years until 1913 when he received his father's inheritance and then moved to Munich.

Hitler was assigned to infiltrate the **German Workers' Party** (DAP), which became the **National Socialist German Workers' Party** or the **Nazi Party** in the same year. His task was to influence other soldiers and monitoring the activities of the DAP. Soon Hitler was attracted to the anti-Semitic, anti-capitalist, nationalist, anti-Marxist ideas of DAP's founder Anton Drexler who also founded the Nazi Party in the following year. Hitler joined DAP in September 1919 becoming the 55th member of the party.

Pan-German or All-German nationalist and anti-Semitic German Workers' Party (DAP) became **Nazi Party** in 1919. Hitler became its chairman in 1921. Hitler's Nazism was inspired by fascism that originated in Italy during the WW I. Nazism rejected any theories of the western capitalism and the Soviet socialism.

Hitler believed in an Aryan German race. Aryan race indicates to an Indo-European (European and Western Asian) Caucasian race and the racist term is used to indicate a white supremacy concept. Hitler also believed in Friedrich Nietzsche's concept of the **Übermensch or 'Super-human'** who should rule above the slave-classes of the **Untermensch or 'inferior humans'**.

Hitler spied on the Nazi Party before joining them:

After participating in WW I, Hitler returned to Munich and remained in the army due to having no formal education or career prospects. He was appointed **Verbindungsmann** or intelligence agent of a reconnaissance commando of Reichswehr in July 1919. Reichswehr was the military organization of Germany from 1919 to 1935. It was united with **Wehrmacht**, the unified armed forces of Germany in 1935.

Chapter - 18

Hitler's Painful Childhood and the Root of his Cruelty

Adolf Hitler was the undisputed leader of Nazi Germany since 1921. Where did the roots of Adolf Hitler's cruelty come from?

Hitler's father, Alois Hitler was a customs officer. Meanwhile, his mother, Klara Hitler, came from a poor peasant family. Financially, the Hitler family lived comfortably.

Alois was a dominating character. And young Adolf often found himself the target of his father's temperament. Alois was an authoritarian, arrogant, domineering, aggressive and cruel figure.

German journalist, Konrad Heiden said, "Hitler's father was a grumpy old man who had struggled fiercely in life. He often made the most difficult sacrifices. And in the end things didn't go the way he wanted them to."

Alois really wanted his son to be successful in life. He didn't hesitate to beat Adolf if he didn't do what he was told. In the book '**He Was My Chief: The Memoirs of Adolf Hitler's Secretary** written by Christa Schroeder, Hitler once told a story: "After reading a book from Karl May, a brave man would show no signs of pain, I decided not to make any sound when I was beaten.".

After that Adolf counted the strokes he got from his father. Adolf proudly told his mother: "Dad hit me 32 times and I didn't cry."

As a child, Adolf Hitler was often sick and his mother became overly protective. She was worried about losing another child. Therefore, Adolf loved his mother very much. He said that one of his happiest memories was sleeping with his mother on the big bed when his father was away.

The bad relationship between Hitler and Alois ended after Alois died on January 3rd 1903. At that time Adolf was 13-years-old and raised by his mother.

His mother raised Hitler by spoiling him. Like her husband, she wanted Adolf to do well in school. Her attempts to persuade Adolf were less successful than her husband's harsh actions. Adolf continued to get poor grades. The gentleness of the mother did not make Adolf show any real interest in his studies.

His last school report, dated September 16th 1905, showed "fair" grades in German, chemistry, physics, geometry and geometric drawings. In geography and history he was "satisfying." However, the drawing of his free hand was described as "extraordinary".

Cruel to sisters

His father's tough attitude descended on Adolf. Two historians, **Timothy Ryback** and **Florian Beierl** found a journal written by Adolf Hitler's sister, Paula Hitler. The journal provides excellent insights into the dysfunctional nature of the Führer family.

Paula Hitler's journal, which was excavated in a secret location in Germany, reveals that her brother was a bully as a teenager. Adolf also did not hesitate to beat Paula.

Recounting the earliest memories of her childhood, when she was about eight and Adolf was 15, Paula wrote: "Once again I felt my brother's hand land on my face."

It is said that scientific tests have verified the authenticity of the document. Paula Hitler, always regarded as the innocent party in the Hitler family, was engaged to one of the Holocaust's most famous euthanasia doctors.

"Adolf is the older brother and father figure. He was very strict with Paula and often slapped him. But Paula confirmed it, because he believed it was for the good of his education," said Dr Ryback.

Adolf's tough attitude continued into adulthood and a character that could not be removed from him. Even though he is now gone, his atrocities with the Holocaust and massive Jewish massacres have left many wounds today.

Chapter – 19

Hitler's Boyhood

(Source: The History Place

https://www.historyplace.com › worldwar2 › boyhood)

In 1895, at age six, two important events happened in the life of young Adolf Hitler. First, the unrestrained, carefree days he had enjoyed up to now came to an end as he entered primary school. Secondly, his father retired on a pension from the Austrian civil service.

This meant a double dose of supervision, discipline and regimentation under the watchful eyes of teachers at school and his strict father at home. His father, now 58, had spent most of his life working his way up through the civil service ranks. He was used to giving orders and having them obeyed and also expected this from his children. The Hitler family lived on a small farm outside of Linz, Austria. The children had farm chores to perform along with their school work.

Hitler's mother was now preoccupied with caring for her new son, Edmund. In 1896, she gave birth to a girl, Paula. The Hitler household now consisted of Adolf, little brother Edmund, little sister Paula, older half-brother Alois Jr., older half-sister Angela and two parents who were home all the time. It was a crowded, noisy little farm house that seems to have gotten on the nerves on Hitler's father who found retirement after 40 years of work to be difficult.

The oldest boy, Alois Jr., 13, bore the brunt of his father's discontent, including harsh words and occasional beatings. A year later, at age 14, young Alois had enough of this treatment and ran away from home, never to see his father again. This put young Adolf, age 7, next in line for the same treatment.

Also at this time, the family moved off the farm to the town of Lambach, Austria, halfway between Linz and Salzburg. This was the first of several moves the family would make during the restless retirement of Hitler's father.

For young Adolf, the move to Lambach meant an end to farm chores and more time to play. There was an old Catholic Benedictine monastery in the town. The ancient monastery was decorated with carved stones and woodwork that included several **swastikas.** Adolf attended school there and saw them every day. They had been put there in the 1800s by the ruling Abbot as a pun or play on words. His name essentially sounded like the German word for swastika, Hakenkreuz.

Young Hitler did well in the monastery school and also took part in the boys' choir. He was said to have had a fine singing voice. Years later Hitler would say the solemn pageantry of the high mass and other Catholic ceremonies was quite intoxicating and left a very deep impression.

As a young boy he idolized the priests and for two years seriously considered becoming a priest himself. He especially admired the Abbot in-charge, who ruled his black-robed monks with supreme authority. At home Hitler sometimes played priest and even included long sermons.

At age nine, he got into schoolboy mischief. He was caught smoking a cigarette by one of the priests, but was forgiven and not punished.

His favorite game to play outside was cowboys and Indians. **Tales of the American West** were very popular among boys in Austria and Germany. Books by **James Fenimore Cooper** and especially German writer **Karl May** were eagerly read and re-enacted. May, who had never been to America, invented a hero named Old Shatterhand, a white man who always won his battles with Native Americans, defeating his enemies through sheer will-power and bravery. Young Hitler read and re-read every one of May's books about Old Shatterhand, totaling more than 70 novels. He continued to read them even as Führer. During the German attack on Soviet Russia, he sometimes referred to the Russians as **Redskins** and ordered his officers to carry May's books about fighting Indians.

In describing his boyhood, Hitler later said of himself that he was an argumentative little ring leader who liked to stay outside and hang around with 'husky' boys. His half-brother Alois later described him as quick to anger and spoiled by his indulgent mother.

In 1898, the Hitler family moved once again, to the village of Leonding, close to Linz. They settled into a small house with a garden located next to a cemetery. This meant another change of schools for Adolf.

He found school easy and got good grades with little effort. He also discovered he had considerable talent for drawing, especially sketching buildings. He had the ability to look at a building, memorize the architectural details, and accurately reproduce it on paper, entirely from memory.

One day, young Hitler went rummaging through his father's book collection and came across several of a military nature, including a picture book on the **War of 1870-71** between the Germans and the French. By Hitler's own account, this book became an obsession. He read it over and over, becoming convinced it had been a glorious event.

"It was not long before the great historic struggle had become my greatest spiritual experience. From then on, I became more and more enthusiastic about everything that was in any was connected with war or, for that matter, with soldiering," Hitler stated in his book **Mein Kampf.**

Cowboys and Indians gave way to battle re-enactments, especially after the **Boer War** broke out in Africa. Hitler, now eleven-years-old, took the side of the Boers against the English and never tired of playing war. Sometimes, he even wore out the boys he was playing with and then simply went and found other boys to continue.

But now at home, tragedy struck. Adolf's little brother Edmund, age 6, died of measles. Adolf, the boy who loved war play and its 'pretend' death now had to confront genuine death for the first time. It seems to have shaken him badly.

To make matters worse, the little boy was buried in the cemetery next to their house. From his bedroom window, Adolf could see the cemetery.

Years later, neighbors recalled that young Adolf was sometimes seen at night sitting on the wall of the cemetery gazing up at the stars.

And there were now more problems for Adolf. His grade school years were coming to an end and he had to choose which type of secondary school to attend, classical or technical. By now, young Hitler had dreams of one day becoming an artist. He wanted to go to the classical school. But his father wanted him to follow in his footsteps and become a civil servant and sent him to the technical high school in the city of Linz, in September 1900.

Hitler, the country boy, was lost in the city and its big school. City kids also looked down on country kids who went to the school. He was very lonely and extremely unhappy. He did quite poorly his first year, getting kept back.

He would later claim he wanted to show his father he was unsuited for technical education with its emphasis on mathematics and science and thus should have been allowed to become an artist.

"I thought that once my father saw what little progress I was making at the [technical school] he would let me devote myself to the happiness I dreamed of," Hitler explained in **Mein Kampf.**

There were frequent arguments at home between young Hitler and his father over his career choice. To the traditional-minded, authoritarian father, the idea of his son becoming an artist seemed utterly ridiculous.

But in the grand scheme of things, as young Adolf saw it, the idea of a career spent sitting in an office all day long doing the boring paperwork of a civil servant was utterly horrible. The dream of becoming an artist seemed to be the answer to all his present day problems.

But his stubborn father refused to listen. And so a bitter struggle began between father and son.

Hitler began his second year at the high school as the oldest boy in his class since he had been kept back. This gave him the advantage over the other boys. Once again he became a little ring leader and even led the boys in afterschool games of cowboys and Indians, becoming Old Shatterhand. He managed to get better grades in his second year, but still failed mathematics.

Another interest of great importance surfaced at this time, German nationalism.

The area of Austria where Hitler grew up is close to the German border. Many Austrians along the border considered themselves to be German-Austrians. Although they were subjects of the Austrian Hapsburg Monarchy and its multicultural empire, they expressed loyalty to the German Imperial House of Hohenzollern and its Kaiser.

In defiance of the Austrian Monarchy, Adolf Hitler and his young friends liked to use the German greeting, **"Heil,"** and sing the German anthem **"Deutschland Über Alles,"** instead of the Austrian Imperial anthem.

Hitler's father had worked as an Austrian Imperial customs agent and continually expressed loyalty to the Hapsburg Monarchy, perhaps unknowingly encouraging his rebellious young son to give his loyalty to the German Kaiser.

There was also a history teacher at school, Dr. Leopold Pötsch, who touched Hitler's imagination with exciting tales of the glory of German figures such as **Bismarck** and **Frederick the Great**. For young Hitler, German nationalism quickly became an obsession. Adding to all this, was another new interest, the operas of German composer, **Richard Wagner.** Hitler saw his first opera at age twelve and was immediately captivated by its Germanic music, pagan myths, tales of ancient Kings and Knights and their glorious struggles against hated enemies.

But now, for young Hitler, the struggle with his father was about to come to a sudden end. In January 1903, Hitler's father died suddenly of a lung hemorrhage, leaving his 13-year-old son as head of the Hitler household.

Copyright © 1996 The History Place™ All Rights Reserved

Chapter - 20

Hitler's Legacy and how it shaped the course of the Modern World

There is no doubt that Hitler indeed left a legacy which shaped the course of the modern world. After the **Third Reich** was reduced to a pile of ashes surrounding Hitler's bunker in Berlin, his story is still the most powerful legacy of violence and hatred mankind has ever seen. The extremism which Adolf Hitler swept at society but in particular German people still frightens many to this day. It is almost impossible to understand how a party based on hatred and hostility towards democracy managed to gain a stranglehold on Europe. Despite Hitler's remarkable capacity for violence and corruption, he rose through the ranks legally through the German political apparatus, becoming **Chancellor** in 1933.

To begin with, World War 2 was about to take place when Adolf Hitler was awarded with great power on August 2, 1934. This power was the title of **Fuhrer of Germany** because President von Hindenburg had just died. Hitler was already Chancellor of Germany and after an agreement with staff at the president's office, Hitler became head of state as well as head of government and was formally named the Führer of Germany. This was tragic as this meant that Hitler had the power to create war at any time he pleased. As a result, Hitler decided to abuse his power and decided to do irresponsible things such as fighting with other countries. He decided to invade the nation of Poland soon after and therefore, other countries got involved and World War 2 began. This war completely changed the course of the modern world

Secondly, there is no doubt that the major event caused by Adolf Hitler which shaped the course of the modern world was the provocation of World War 2. World War 2 started when Hitler decided to undertake the invasion of Poland on September 1, 1939. Two days later, France and Britain declared war on Germany, beginning World War II. Over the next six years, this conflict took more lives and destroyed more land and property around the globe than any previous war which took place. Among the estimated 45-60 million people killed, there were 6 million Jews murdered in Nazi concentration camps as part of Hitler's diabolical **"Final Solution,"** now known as the Holocaust.

As a result of Hitler's creation of World War 2, Europe's hierarchy was also destroyed. The countries and nations of Britain, France, Belgium and the Netherlands all lost their empires due to the devastating result World War 2 had on most countries. The main devastating result of the war was that these countries lost their energy and wealth to maintain their power after all the fighting that took place. After the war, Europe faced the task of rebuilding many of it's broken buildings. After all this chaos Hitler actually wanted peace with the British so he could completely demolish the Soviets. Britain kindly denied this deal because they didn't trust in Hitler's promise. Britain simply couldn't bet their nation on Hitler's word.

Additionally, Hitler also cost Europe their religious beliefs. It is startling, the extent to which Christian Europe had abandoned Christianity for secularism. After the war, the decline of church attendance raised to levels never seen before. It was not just Hitler who destroyed Europe's religious aspect but in many ways it destroyed itself from the inside. Christianity in Europe was already on the decline but the contribution which Hitler had was that he was the provider of a **coup de grace**. After World War 2 ended, irreversible damage to Europe's religious beliefs occurred as they believed that religion causes outrageous views and therefore cause war to take place.

The final and most relieving impact Adolf Hitler made on the world was his death. Hitler committed suicide by a gunshot in his bunker on the 30th of April 1945. This bunker was situated in Berlin and was used as a raid shelter during World War 2. The death of Adolf Hitler was very significant and pleased the majority of those alive at the time both positively and negatively. The majority of people in society were all relieved when Adolf Hitler died as he was responsible and caused over 80 million deaths. The world changed the day he died, as there was no need to worry about an evil dictator as powerful as Hitler.

Kershaw describes Hitler as "the embodiment of modern political evil". "Never in history has such ruination—physical and moral—been associated with the name of one man", he adds. Hitler's political programme brought about a world war, leaving behind a devastated and impoverished Eastern and Central Europe. Germany suffered wholesale destruction, characterised as **Stunde Null (Zero Hour)**. Hitler's policies inflicted human suffering on an unprecedented scale; according to **R. J. Rummel**, the Nazi regime was responsible for the democidal killing of an estimated 19.3 million civilians and prisoners of war. In addition, 28.7 million soldiers and civilians died as a result of military action in the European theatre of World War II. The number of civilians killed during the Second World War was unprecedented in the history of warfare. Historians, philosophers, and politicians often use the word "evil" to describe the Nazi regime. Many European countries have criminalised both the promotion of Nazism and Holocaust denial.

Historian **Friedrich Meinecke** described Hitler as "one of the great examples of the singular and incalculable power of personality in historical life". English historian **Hugh Trevor-Roper** saw him as "among the 'terrible simplifiers' of history, the most systematic, the most historical, the most philosophical, and yet the coarsest, cruelest, least magnanimous conqueror the world has ever known". For historian **John M. Roberts**, Hitler's defeat marked the end of a phase of European history dominated by Germany. In its place emerged the Cold War, a global confrontation between the Western Bloc, dominated by the United States and other NATO nations, and the Eastern Bloc, dominated by the Soviet Union. Historian **Sebastian Haffner** asserts that without Hitler and the displacement of the Jews, the modern nation state of Israel would not exist. He contends that without Hitler, the de-colonisation of former European spheres of influence would have been postponed. Further, Haffner claims that other than Alexander the Great, Hitler had a more significant impact than any other comparable historical figure, in that he too caused a wide range of worldwide changes in a relatively short time span.

Chapter – 21

Downfall of Adolf Hitler

(Source: The History Place

https://www.historyplace.com › worldwar2 › downfall)

All his life, Adolf Hitler had been obsessed with the musical works of German composer, Richard Wagner. As a teenager living in Austria, Hitler was deeply inspired by Wagner's operas and their pagan, mythical tales of struggles against hated enemies. One time, back in 1905, after seeing Wagner's opera Rienzi, young Hitler professed he would someday embark on a great mission, leading his people to freedom, similar to the opera's story.

Now, some 40 years later, after failing in his mission as Führer of the German People and Reich, another of Wagner's operas hearkened, and it was Hitler's favorite – **Der Ring des Nibelungen**. It concerns a magic Ring granting its possessor the power to rule the world. In the last part of this opera, entitled **Götterdämmerung** or **'Twilight of the gods,"** the hero Siegfried, betrayed by those around him, loses the Ring and winds up on a funeral pyre while the fortress of Valhalla burns and the kingdom of the gods is destroyed.

This essentially was the ending Hitler inflicted upon himself, his People and his Reich.

Piece by piece, it all came together over the last ten days of his life, beginning on Friday, April 20, 1945. That day Hitler met for the last time with his top Nazis. The occasion was Hitler's 56th birthday, a dreary celebration inside the Führerbunker in Berlin. Present were Joseph Goebbels, Hermann Göring, Heinrich Himmler, Joachim Ribbentrop, Albert Speer and Martin Bormann, along with military leaders Wilhelm Keitel, Alfred Jodl, Karl Dönitz, and Hans Krebs, the new Chief of the General Staff.

At first, those present tried to convince the Führer to leave doomed Berlin for the relative safety of Berchtesgaden, the mountain area along the German-Austrian border where he had his villa. From there he could continue the fight, supported by troops positioned throughout the impenetrable Alpine mountains of western Austria and southern Bavaria. Such a move might prolong the war indefinitely and improve the odds of a favorable outcome for Germany, one way or another.

But Hitler brushed aside this suggestion, knowing that any journey outside the bunker brought great risk of capture. And above all, the Führer did not want himself, alive or dead, to wind up prominently displayed by his enemies, particularly the Russians. However, he did give his bunker personnel permission to leave. Most of his staff therefore departed for Berchtesgaden via a convoy of trucks and planes, still hoping the Führer would follow. Only a handful of Hitler's personal staff remained with him, including his top aide Martin Bormann, a few SS and military aides, two private secretaries, and his longtime companion, Eva Braun.

Hitler's choice to remain in the Führerbunker to the very end amounted to his final decision of the war. It was made known to the German people via a special radio announcement in the hope that his presence in the Nazi capital would inspire all remaining Wehrmacht, SS, Volkssturm and Hitler Youth units in Berlin to hold out to the end as well.

Although the war was lost, Hitler nevertheless took pride in the knowledge that he had not allowed another repeat of November 1918, when the German Army had meekly asked the Allies for armistice terms to conclude the First World War. This was all Hitler had left. Just a few years earlier, the Führer had been regarded by most German's as their greatest-ever military leader. Now, all that remained of his military legacy was the fact he had refused to give up no matter what.

The Führer's stubborn pride insured that thousands of German soldiers, Hitler Youths and civilians would needlessly lose their lives in the streets of Berlin, where advance units of the Red Army were already probing. Inside the bunker, Hitler told General Jodl, "I will fight as long as I have a single soldier. When the last soldier deserts me. I will shoot myself."

However, the Führer's fatalism was not shared by his two oldest comrades, Hermann Göring and Heinrich Himmler, who had both scooted away from Berlin just hours after Hitler's birthday gathering. Göring made it safely to Berchtesgaden where he had his own villa, bringing along truckloads of artworks looted from museums all over occupied Europe. For his part, Himmler headed in the opposite direction, staying for the moment in a small town northwest of Berlin.

Both men were spurred to act on their own in the aftermath of the Führer's shocking behavior during the military conference held in the bunker on Sunday, April 22nd. To everyone there that day, it seemed the Führer had suffered a total mental and physical breakdown, completely losing control while letting loose a shrieking denunciation of the Army, then collapsing into a chair. News of the Führer's appalling condition spread like wildfire among the top Nazis outside Berlin, including Göring and Himmler.

Göring, the Führer's designated successor, now pondered whether or not to announce he was the new leader of the Reich, since Hitler was presently cut off from the rest of Germany in besieged Berlin, and apparently incapacitated. But the inherent danger of such a move, even at this late stage, gave him pause for concern. And so Göring put off a decision and instead sent Hitler a carefully worded telegram the next day, Monday, April 23rd, trying to feel him out:

"My Führer! In view of your decision to remain in the fortress of Berlin, do you agree that I take over at once the total leadership of the Reich, with full freedom of action at home and abroad as your deputy, in accordance with your decree of June 29, 1941? If no reply is received by 10 o'clock tonight, I shall take it for granted that you have lost your freedom of action, and shall consider the conditions of your decree as fulfilled, and shall act for the best interests of our country and our people..."

Göring didn't know that Hitler had since rebounded from his meltdown and regained a measure of composure. Therefore, Hitler's response to Göring's telegram, prompted by Martin Bormann, was that the Reich Marshal had committed "high treason." Although this carried the death penalty, Göring would be spared if he immediately resigned all of his titles and offices – which Göring promptly did. Next, Bormann, a longtime behind-the-scenes foe of Göring, transmitted an order to the SS near Berchtesgaden to arrest Göring and his staff. As a result, just before dawn on Tuesday, April 24, Göring was put under house arrest. Thus ended the long career of the man who would be Führer.

In contrast to Göring's cautiousness, Himmler took a much bolder approach. At the very moment that Hitler was reading Göring's telegram, Himmler was secretly proposing the surrender all German troops in the West to General Eisenhower.

Himmler had traveled to the city of Lübeck in northern Germany to meet with Count Folke Bernadotte of the Swedish Red Cross. Himmler's idea was to have Bernadotte contact Eisenhower regarding the surrender in the West, while at the same time Germany would continue fighting the Russians in the East, soon to be joined by the Americans and British. Playing a key role in this new German-American-British alliance would be the leader of post-Hitler Germany, Heinrich Himmler himself.

His proposal got nowhere. By now, Himmler's name, and that of the SS organization he headed, was already synonymous with mass murder.

Meanwhile, the military situation continued to deteriorate. On Wednesday, April 25th, Russian and American soldiers greeted each other face-to-face at Torgau on the Elbe River, seventy-five miles south of Berlin, effectively severing Nazi Germany in two. The next day, Russian artillery fire made the first direct hits upon the Reich Chancellery buildings in Berlin and the grounds directly above the Führerbunker.

A German tank officer described the scene in his diary: "We retreat again under heavy Russian air attacks. Inscriptions [I see] on house walls [say]: 'The hour before sunrise is darkest' and 'We retreat but we are winning.'... The night is fiery red. Heavy shelling. Otherwise a terrible silence...Women and children huddling in niches and corners and listening for the sounds of battle...Nervous breakdowns."

By Friday, April 27, Russian bombardment of the Reich Chancellery buildings had reached its peak with numerous direct hits, causing Hitler to send frantic telegrams to Field Marshal Keitel demanding that Berlin be relieved by now non-existent armies.

For Hitler, the worst blow of all came the next day when BBC news radio reports concerning Himmler's surrender negotiations were broadcast from London and picked up by Goebbels' Propaganda Ministry. According to eyewitnesses in the bunker, Hitler "raged like a madman" with a ferocity never seen before when informed of the betrayal. Himmler had been at his side since the beginning, earning the fond nickname Der Treue Heinrich (Faithful Heinrich) through years of murderous, fanatical service to his Führer. Now, Hitler wanted to have him shot.

Since Himmler was nowhere to be found, Hitler ordered his personal liaison in the bunker, SS-General Hermann Fegelein, shot instead. Fegelein was already under suspicion, having been nabbed the day before trying to sneak out of Berlin in civilian clothing. After some brief questioning, he was taken up to the Chancellery garden above the bunker and summarily executed.

In the meantime, advance units of the Red Army had smashed through the German defenses in Berlin and were only a few miles away from the bunker. Hitler was informed there was perhaps a day or two left before the Russians arrived at his doorstep.

Now, at long last, Hitler reconciled himself to defeat, and began preparations for his own death.

First, he married Eva Braun, as a reward for her ceaseless devotion, during a relationship in which she had spent nearly all of her time at Berchtesgaden waiting for him to show up. They were married in a brief ceremony about an hour past midnight, early Sunday, April 29, with Goebbels and Bormann in attendance. Everyone was then invited into the Führer's private quarters for a wedding breakfast featuring champagne and fond reminisces by Hitler of better days gone by, followed by a bitter accounting of the recent betrayal by his two oldest comrades. Those who listened were moved to tears. Shortly thereafter, Hitler excused himself, bringing along his staff secretary, Traudl Junge, to whom he dictated his last will along with a two-part political testament.

In his will he left his possessions to the Nazi Party and also revealed his fate: "I myself and my wife – in order to escape the disgrace of deposition or capitulation – choose death. It is our wish to be burnt immediately on the spot where I have carried out the greatest part of my daily work in the course of twelve years' of service to my people."

His political testament recited familiar themes first stated in his book **'Mein Kampf'** back in 1925. In addition, he blamed the Jews for everything, including the war. He cited the extermination threat he had made on January 30, 1939, followed by a veiled reference to the gas chambers, labeling them a "humane means" of making the Jews atone for the guilt of causing the war.

In the second part of his political testament, he expelled both Göring and Himmler from the Nazi Party and appointed Admiral Karl Dönitz as his successor, not as Führer, but as President of the Reich. Dönitz was to preside over a government with Goebbels as Chancellor and Bormann as Party Minister. After completing his dictations, Hitler went off to bed, having been up all night.

While the Führer slept, the **Battle of Berlin** raged in the streets above him, with the Germans fighting fanatically to defend every inch, just as Hitler hoped they would. Above all, they tried to knock out the Russian T34 tanks now rolling toward Hitler. A Russian tank driver recalled: "There were a lot of Panzerfausts [anti-tank grenade launchers] in Berlin. They were lying in every basement. Mostly the operators were old men or boys."

Casualties on both sides were high. But the Russians pressed forward relentlessly, blasting through anything in their way. The Red Army under Marshal Zhukov, after a journey of some 1500 miles that had begun back in Stalingrad, was now close to victory. When the Führer awoke about noontime, he was told that Russian troops were only a mile from the bunker.

The Chancellery garden with entrance to the Führerbunker on left and adjacent ventilation tower as seen in 1947. Below: Portrait from 1942 of Eva Braun and Hitler with his dog Blondi.

Realizing their Führer intended to self-destruct, four of his remaining military adjutants asked for permission to leave the bunker, on the excuse that they wanted to check on the status of a relief column supposedly being led by General Wenck. Hitler granted their requests. He also took this opportunity to give his Luftwaffe adjutant, Colonel Below, one last Führer message to be hand delivered to the Army High Command:

"The people and the armed forces have given their all in this long and hard struggle. The sacrifice has been enormous. But my trust has been misused by many people. Disloyalty and betrayal have undermined resistance throughout the war. It was therefore not granted to me to lead the people to victory. The Army General Staff cannot be compared with the General Staff in the First World War. Its achievements were far behind those of the fighting front. The efforts and sacrifices of the German people in this war have been so great that I cannot believe that they have been in vain. The aim must still be to win territory in the East for the German people."

Thus the last official words of the Führer contained both a final insult of the Army leadership along with a repetition of the Lebensraum theme for the East.

Shortly thereafter, the final bit of news from the outside world ever to reach Hitler told of the death of his oldest political ally, Benito Mussolini. The one-time dictator of Italy had tried to flee along with his mistress, but had been captured by Italian partisans, executed, hung upside down and then thrown into the gutter. Hitler's only reaction was an expressed determination not to suffer a similar fate.

Hitler never heard the other news that day from Italy. SS-General Karl Wolff, formerly Himmler's chief aide, had successfully negotiated the unconditional surrender of all German forces in Italy to the Western Allies.

Hitler's sole concern right now was to ready himself for the moment of death. He had in his possession several small glass capsules containing liquid cyanide poison. All one had to do was bite down on the glass and painless death would follow in seconds. But since the capsules had been supplied by the now-traitorous Himmler, the Führer worried they might not be the real thing. Hitler therefore ordered one tested on his favorite dog, Blondi, which killed the animal instantly. After this, he handed out the cyanide capsules to his female secretaries, apologizing that he did not have better parting gifts for them. The capsules, he told them, were theirs to use when the Russians stormed the bunker.

As Sunday evening wore on, Hitler asked everyone to stay up. They waited for hours, for what they sensed would be a final goodbye. It came about 2:30 a.m., early in the morning of Monday, April 30th, when Hitler came out of his private quarters into the dining area. The remaining members of his staff lined up to receive him. With glazed eyes, Hitler shook each hand, muttering a few inaudible words quietly, then retired back into his quarters. His secretary, Traudl Junge, recalled the moment: "He looked like a shadow. He looked emotionless, and very gray and pale, like a broken old

   The Rise Of Adolf Hitler

man...his movements were very slow. He was not the dictator anymore, and the impressive, fascinating man he was earlier."

Following the Führer's departure, his staff mulled over the significance of what they had just experienced. Strangely, the tremendous tension of preceding days seemed to suddenly evaporate upon their realization that the end was near. A lighthearted mood surfaced, followed by spontaneous displays of merry-making even including dancing. At one point, they had to be told to keep the noise down.

At noontime on April 30th, Hitler attended his last-ever military conference and was told the Russians were a block away. Two hours later, Hitler sat down for his final meal, a vegetarian lunch. His wife had no appetite. In the meantime, his chauffeur was ordered to deliver 200 liters of gasoline to the Chancellery garden.

Hitler, accompanied by his wife Eva, now bid a last farewell to Bormann, Goebbels, Generals Krebs and Burgdorf. Hitler and his wife went back into their private quarters while Bormann and Goebbels stood quietly nearby. A few moments later, about 3:30 p.m., a gunshot was heard. Bormann and Goebbels hesitated at first, then entered the room. They saw the body of Hitler sprawled on the sofa, dripping with blood from a gunshot to his right temple. He had killed himself with the same small revolver he once used to fire a warning shot into the ceiling back during the Beer Hall Putsch in November 1923 – a gun he had kept ever since. His wife, Eva, had died from biting into one of the cyanide capsules.

As Russian artillery shells exploded nearby, the bodies were carried up the stairs to the Reich Chancellery garden, placed in a shell crater, doused heavily with gasoline and burned while Bormann and Goebbels stood by silently, with arms extended in a final Nazi salute. Over the next three hours, the bodies were repeatedly doused until there were only charred remains, which were swept into a canvas, laid in a different shell crater and buried anonymously.

Back inside the bunker, with the Führer now gone, people lit cigarettes, a practice Hitler had forbidden in his presence. Next, they began to organize themselves into groups to flee the bunker and hopefully escape the Russians.

For Joseph Goebbels, life without Hitler was not worth living for himself, his wife and their six young children. On Tuesday, May 1st, Goebbels and his wife therefore poisoned their six children, aged 12 and younger, whom they had brought into the bunker. Next they went up into the Chancellery garden and each bit into a cyanide capsule. After collapsing and dying, they were shot in the head by an SS man as Goebbels had requested. Their bodies were then burned, but only partially, and were not buried. The macabre remains were discovered by the Russians the next day and filmed, with the grotesquely charred body of Goebbels becoming an enduring symbol of the legacy of Hitler's twelve-year Reich.

At 10 p.m. on May 1st, a special radio announcement told the German people their Führer had died "fighting with his last breath for Germany against Bolshevism," and also announced Dönitz as his designated successor. By now, the Russians were already combing through the wreckage of the Reich Chancellery looking for any sign of Hitler's body.

With the Führer dead and the German nation in ruins, Dönitz and surviving leaders of the Wehrmacht had just one thing in mind – stall for time to allow as many troops and civilians as possible to flee from the Russians and make it into western zones occupied by the Americans and British.

Thus it wasn't until Saturday, May 5th, when a military representative, Admiral Hans von Friedeburg, was sent by Dönitz to General Eisenhower's headquarters at Reims, France. He was then joined by General Jodl. Even now, the Germans tried to stall the proceedings by suggesting a piecemeal surrender limited to the West, thereby allowing even more troops to flee the Russians. But Eisenhower saw through this ploy and demanded the Germans quit stalling and sign an unconditional surrender for all fronts.

And so, in the early morning hours of Monday, May 7th, with authorization from Dönitz, General Jodl signed the unconditional surrender document. The signing was, as Winston Churchill put it, "the signal for the greatest outburst of joy in the history of mankind." Huge crowds gathered to rejoice in London, Paris, New York and Moscow.

The guns across Europe were silent. Nazi Germany was finished.

The German people, who had once cheered mightily for Hitler and enthusiastically embraced Nazism, now faced a stark and uncertain future. A German woman summed up the dilemma: "There won't be any more dying, any more raids. It's over. But then the fear set in of what would happen afterwards. We were spiritually and emotionally drained. Hitler's doctrines were discredited. And then the desperation set in of realizing that it had all been for nothing, and that was a terrible feeling. Surviving, finding something to eat and drink, was less difficult for me than the psychological emptiness. It was incomprehensible that all this was supposed to be over, and that it had all been for nothing."

For Jews and others, who had been targeted by Nazis, a great sense of relief was felt at outlasting Hitler. One woman who survived the Final Solution reflected: "During the five terrible war years, we could not indulge in simple pleasures that life offers to normal people. All our efforts were directed towards fighting the enemy and surviving. Now, for the first time since September 1, 1939, we could unwind and be normal again – to walk the streets without the fear of hearing the hated "Halt!" without the fear of being rounded up by the Germans and pushed into military trucks. No more "Achtung, Achtung!" coming down from the street loud-speakers. No more ghettos, no more starvation, typhus, gas chambers, Einsatzgruppen [killing squads]. The intense fear and persecution were over."

The Germans themselves had paid dearly for Hitler's war, suffering four million civilian and three million military deaths. Hitler's nemesis, Soviet Russia, had suffered staggering losses including seven million soldiers and an estimated 16 million civilian deaths. Throughout Europe and Russia, six million Jews had been systematically murdered by Nazis.

For the victorious Allies, with images of recently liberated concentration camps still fresh in their minds, the question of justice now arose. Fortunately for the Allies, the rapid demise of Nazi Germany had resulted in the wholesale capture of gigantic document archives from all branches of Hitler's government along with secret papers, conference reports and private diaries.

The Nazis had kept meticulous written records of their activities, from mass murder of the Jews, to Hitler's private talks. In addition, captured Nazi officials and high ranking military officers underwent lengthy interrogations. With all of the evidence at hand, the Allies decided to prosecute. The place chosen for the trial was Nuremberg, the now-ruined city that had once hosted annual rallies glorifying Hitler and Nazism.

(Copyright © 2010 The History Place™ All Rights Reserved)

Chapter - 22

Best books and films about Hitler's death

Given below are some of the best books and films, fiction and non-fiction, dealing with Hitler's death.

1. The Last Days of Hitler - Hugh Trevor Roper

After the war came to an end, the circumstances surrounding Adolf Hitler's death remained mysterious. An official statement had been broadcast by Admiral Doenitz, Hitler's personally appointed successor, maintaining that the Führer had died with this troops in Berlin. Despite this, rumours that Hitler had escaped began to circulate, with the architect of the final solution being variously said to be hiding out in a Spanish monastery, living on a ranch in South America or even holed up with bandits in the mountains of Albania.

By September 1945, Hitler had been missing for four months and the allies were anxious to establish the precise details of Hitler's death and appointed a British intelligence officer to discover the truth. Before the war, Hugh Trevor-Roper had been a brilliant classicist at Oxford University. During the conflict, his analytical mind had found a fresh outlet cracking codes at Bletchley Park and interpreting raw intelligence data, now it was put to work ascertaining 'the personal fate of Hitler', as he put it.

His meticulous investigation proved beyond reasonable doubt that Hitler had killed himself in his bunker. Invited to turn his findings into a book, he produced one of the most vital and compelling works of history ever written.

First published in 1947, **The Last Days of Hitler** has remained in print ever since, and it provides a gripping picture of the lunatic disintegration of the Third Reich.

2. Inside Hitler's Bunker - Joachim Fest

Joachim Fest was six when Hitler came to power and an 18-year-old prisoner of war when the Führer committed suicide. Born in Berlin to a well-educated Catholic middle-class family who utterly rejected Hitler and National Socialism from the moment they first appeared, Fest, a journalist and newspaper editor and publisher, would pen one of the first major biographies of Adolf Hitler in Germany.

Written in the wake of the fall of the Berlin Wall and with access to some eyewitness accounts that were unavailable to Trevor-Roper, Third **Inside Hitler's Bunker: the last day of the Reich** vividly recreates what was happening in the bunker, as well as in the German capital as hopes faded and the city went down in a maelstrom of destruction.

3. Until the Final Hour: Hitler's Last Secretary - Traudl Junge

Written in 1947 but not published until shortly before her death in 2002, **Until the Final Hour** offers an intimate, domestic portrait of life in Hitler's inner circle from Traudl Junge, who acted as his secretary from 1942 and was in the bunker when he committed suicide.

4. The End: Germany, 1944-45 - Ian Kershaw

In **The End**, the historian Ian Kershaw recounts the story of the German war from the aftermath of the failed attempt to assassinate Hitler in July 1944 until end of May 1945, when the Führer was deemed missing or dead, and his successors were arrested and their government dissolved.

A catalogue of the appalling human suffering to befall those caught up in the war's final chapter, it considers just why so many Germans remained loyal to Hitler and kept fighting right up until the bitter end.

5. Running Dog - Don DeLillo

Don DeLillo's brilliantly inventive and savagely funny 1978 novel **Running Dog** concerns the discovery of a fragment of pornographic film purportedly shot in a bunker in the climactic days of Berlin's fall – with Hitler as its star.

Films

1. Der Letzte Akt (The Last Ten Days, 1955) - Director: G. W. Pabst

Filmed in Austria just a decade after the war, and directed by G. W. Pabst, one of Germany's most inventive moviemakers before Hitler's rise to power, and with a script by Erich Maria Remarque, author of All Quiet on the Western Front, **The Last Ten Days** was one of the earliest native attempts to dramatise Hitler's response to the crumbling of his insane ambitions. The film was later remade in English as Hitler: The Last Ten Days in 1973 with Alec Guinness in the lead role.

2. Blind Spot: Hitler's Secretary - Directors: Andre Heller and Othmar Schmiderer

This austerely shot 90-minute Austrian documentary was drawn from over 13 hours of interviews with Traudl Junge, one of Hitler's secretaries. In it, she relates the often mundane realities of serving right at the heart of the Third Reich, though seemingly oblivious to the extent of the evil it was perpetrating.

3. Downfall- Director: Oliver Hirschbiegel

Downfall provides a captivating cinematic exploration of the concluding days of Hitler's life. Set almost entirely inside the Berlin bunker, and based on the memoir by Hitler's secretary, Traudl Junge and Joachim Fest's study of Hitler's demise, the film boasts an astonishing performance by Bruno Ganz as the Führer coming to terms with his impending defeat.

*****